The Mountain Pocket ok

Written by Alan Crosby *Foreword by Eric Langmuir*

CORDEE

The Mountain Pocket Book
First Edition

Alan Crosby hereby asserts and gives notice of his right under section 77 of the Copyright, Designs & Patents Act 1988 to be identified as the author of this work.

Copyright © Alan Crosby 1999
Reprinted with revisions 2002

ISBN: 1 871890 78 0

British Library Cataloguing Publication Data
A catalogue record for this book is available from the British Library

Every effort has been made to ensure that the information in this book is as accurate as possible. Like the mountains, information and techniques can change very rapidly. No legal liability is accepted for any accident or damages sustained for whatever reason.

This book is available from all specialist equipment shops and booksellers. Please write for a copy of the comprehensive Cordee stocklist of outdoor recreation and travel books and maps.

Cordee, 3a De Montfort Street, Leicester, LE1 7HD

Printed and bound in Great Britain by
Technographics. Colchester. Essex

For Helen Cunningham

Acknowledgements

The basis of my interest in mountaineering has been the Duke of Edinburgh's Award Scheme (D of E) and my years in the Army. I am particularly grateful to Ian Wilson my best mate at school and to Dave Hall, French teacher and D of E instructor at Richmond Secondary Modern School in Whitehaven. (Now sadly closed.)

Researching this book has lead me on an interesting journey of rediscovery. I owe a great deal to the many individuals with whom I have come into contact over the years.

Thanks also to Paul Warsdale for a lot of the art work (with help from his sister Ella and Ian Mayor). To Kathryn Smith for advice on design and layout, and to Steve Bailey for his invaluable assistance with section 1.3.

I also acknowledge the helpful comments and observations of my fellow Officers and men of the NGS Troop, 289 Cdo Bty RA (V).

Thank you also to Roy and Lorraine Grundy, Carl Pryce and Rosie Hickie. To Rob Howard my editor for his invaluable advice and assistance.

Alan Crosby was educated at Whitehaven Grammar School in Cumbria and the Royal Military Academy Sandhurst (RMAS). He has a BSc (Hons) in Environmental Studies, and an MSc in Environmental Technology from the Imperial College of Science, Technology and Medicine in London.

He has a life long interest in mountaineering and has experience throughout the UK, Norway, the Alps and Nepal. He is also an expedition instructor with the Duke of Edinburgh's Award Scheme in Berkshire.

Contents

Section 3. Hazardous Terrain

Section 4. Winter

4.1. Snow Condition

4.2. Avalanche

4.3. Avalanche Survival

Section 5. Actions If !

Section 6. First Aid

6.1. The Essentials

6.2. Cold & Heat Injuries

Section 7. Access

Appendices

Illustration Credits

The following illustrations are by Paul (Peaky) Warsdale. All others are by the author.

Section 1. 1.1.3. 1.1.4. 1.4.7. 1.4.8.
Section 3. 3.1.4, 3.1.6, 3.1.7, 3.1.8, 3.1.10 - 3.1.12, 3.2.5, 3.2.7 - 3.2.12. 3.3.5 - 3.3.9.
Section 4. 4.1.2, 4.1.9, 4.1.10, 4.2.2, 4.2.3.
Section 5. 5.1, 5.2, 5.4.
Section 6. 6.1.8, 6.1.9, 6.2.2.

Foreword

One of the criticisms of "Mountaincraft and Leadership" I hear from time to time is that it is far too bulky to carry in your rucksack, let alone your hip pocket. Well, here is a little book which will delight those who like to have all the relevant facts and figures at their finger tips.

"The Mountain Pocket Book" is a veritable mine of information dealing with almost every aspect of hillwalking and mountaineering techniques in the British Isles. However, the practice of mountaineering is not writ in tablets of stone and Alan Crosby rightly recognises the dangers in slavishly following the written word and advocates a flexible and questioning approach to the material.

Sound technique is important and tables and weather reports have their place, but at the end of the day the qualities which make the finest mountaineers are human ones; imagination, adaptability, good judgement and a liberal dose of common sense. None of these can be acquired by reading, but what reading can do is to inspire participation, to heighten appreciation and to guide progress in the acquisition of skills.

This book admirably fulfills the latter role, particularly for those who already have some experience of hillwalking and can put the techniques described into their proper context.

Eric Langmuir.

Introduction

This book is designed to stimulate discussion and positive criticism of the subject matter. As techniques and methods change and develop we should be in a position to test and evaluate those ideas for ourselves and make our own judgements. It will be of use to all who venture into the great outdoors, expert or casual users, there is something here for every one.

Positive feedback, suggestions, ideas and criticism of this book are actively encouraged. Never let an "expert" tell you that there is only one way to do things. Be very cautious and suspicious of anyone who refuses to listen to your point of view and ideas. Be doubly wary of anyone who refuses to accept criticism or questioning.

Each section contains an abridged account of technique and method. At the end of the book is the reference section and further reading lists, these should be referred to if you wish to have a deeper understanding of the subject matter.

How to use this book

This book is probably best used as a "dip in and check" reference book. It is designed to be carried in your pocket or rucksack and is no substitute for practical experience.

It is recommended that you are aware of its content before you venture out. Revise and question it continuously and try to test the facts. For instance, compare weather forecasts with what actually happens on your route. Count your calories and note the effects of varying mixes of fats and carbohydrates. Continuously reevaluate your pacing and timings.

Try to amend the tables for your own use. For instance you may be fitter than the general average so your pacing and timing tables may be quite different from the examples in the book. You may be able to survive on far fewer calories, so adjust the tables accordingly.

If you are leading a group on any sort of activity use the book to question and enhance their understanding too. The book is of particular use to MLTB and SMLTB candidates alike.

1. Planning

1.0. Introduction

A little planning and forethought really does go a long way.
These three rules of thumb are very useful no matter what the
situation.

- **KISS - K**eep **I**t **S**imple **S**tupid

- **No plan survives contact with reality,** so be prepared, stay
  flexible and keep your sense of humour

- **The 7 P's**
    - **P**rior
    - **P**lanning &
    - **P**reparation
    - **P**revents
    - **P**   *Use your own word*
    - **P**oor
    - **P**erformance

This book is for guidance only, you are advised to amend detail to
fit your own requirements.

We are responsible for our own actions, in a group there will not
always be a "leader", we are all equally responsible and should
ensure that we are equipped and prepared for each trip. Of course,
we should also look after each other too.

1.1. Time & Space

1.1.0. Introduction

Having decided to venture out there are some considerations which should be made to get maximum enjoyment from the day. The first is available daylight in which to make the trip. A night time journey can be an enjoyable challenge too, but consult the moon state tables found in some of the broadsheet newspapers.

Once we know how much daylight is available we can start looking at the route for length, height gain and potential difficulties. Consideration is also given to the group, general state of fitness and experience. From this we can now work out how long the route should take and whether it is practical for the group.

At annex D are some kit lists which you may like to consider, no suggestion is made about what to carry as this decision depends on a great many factors.

A sound appreciation of the weather is also vital. Strong wind and rain in our faces at the end of the day will present a whole range of problems, not least of which is morale. If there is going to be adverse weather it is worth amending your plans to avoid potential problems caused by a tired group walking into foul weather at the end of the day with fading light.

1.1.1. UK Sun Rise & Sun Set Tables

Latitude 52°N includes the whole of Southern England, Wales and the Peak District. Latitude 56°N includes Northern England, Northern Ireland & Scotland.

Sun rise is when the top edge of the sun first breaks the horizon. Sun set is when the top edge finally drops over the horizon. Dusk is the period of increasing light before the sun rises and failing light after the sun has set. Available light is greatly influenced by prevailing weather conditions and your location.

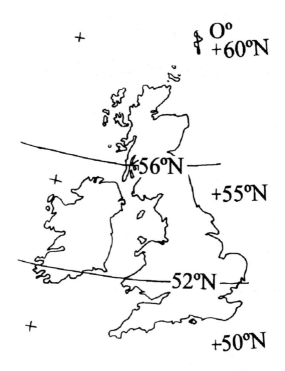

Times (GMT) are for the mid point of the month.

Month	52°N			56°N		
	Rise	**Set**	**Dusk**	**Rise**	**Set**	**Dusk**
January	0800	1618	40	0820	1558	45
February	0721	1708	35	0730	1700	39
March	0613	1806	35	0614	1805	39
April	0504	1857	35	0455	1906	40
May	0405	1949	41	0346	2008	41
June	0340	2019	48	0314	2045	61
July	0408	2004	35	0347	2025	40
August	0452	1914	37	0440	1925	42
September	0537	1811	34	0535	1813	37
October	0624	1707	34	0631	1700	38
November	0726	1604	38	0744	1546	43
December	0803	1549	41	0827	1525	47

1.1.2. Group Size - Ratios (Leader : Group)

It is sensible to consider carefully the number of people that any leader should be expected to safely cope with, no matter how experienced or well qualified they are.

The following organisations issue guidelines about ratios of instructors or leaders to students. These guidelines are included here as examples of good practice.

The Mountain Walking Leader Training Board (MLTB) providers of Mountain Leader Training and Assessment Courses are required to have ratios of 1 instructor : 6 Students. Or 1: 4 for more technical or hazardous activity such as night navigation, rope work and security on steep ground.

Glenmore Lodge (The Scottish National Mountain Sports Centre) stipulate ratios in their courses brochure. Examples are; winter hill walking 1:8, winter mountain craft 1:4 for technical session and 1:6 at all other times.

Plas Y Brenin (The National Mountain Centre) operates on similar ratios to Glenmore Lodge.

The Duke Of Edinburgh's Award (D of E) stipulates a maximum of 7 in the group.

Notes on party leadership are at annex G

1.1.3. Slope Steepness & Snow

The table below indicates how much time to add to your plan for short sections of steep ground. As illustrated if you are going up a 40° slope increase your time by 40%. Snow is a modifying factor for both flat terrain and on a hill.

For both situations

- For soft ankle deep snow add 20% to your time estimate.
- For soft snow up to knee deep add 40% to your time estimate.
- For snow over knee deep double your time estimate.

e.g. On a 40° slope in knee deep snow - add 40% for the slope and 40% for the snow. So if your time estimate is 1 hour for this section add 24 mins for the slope and 24 mins for the snow. The new time estimate is 1 hour 48 mins. Do not under estimate the effect of slope and snow. See Section 4, Winter.

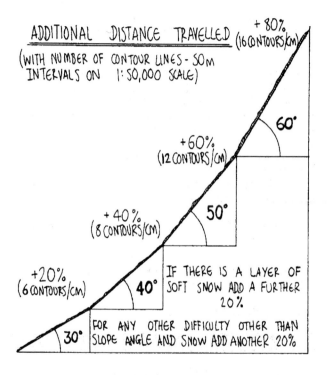

1.1.4. Estimating Slope By Hand Angles

The easiest visual method for estimating the angle of a slope is by using hand angles. The method requires that the user is estimating angles frequently because it only works when slopes are in profile. Head on estimation is not possible using this method.

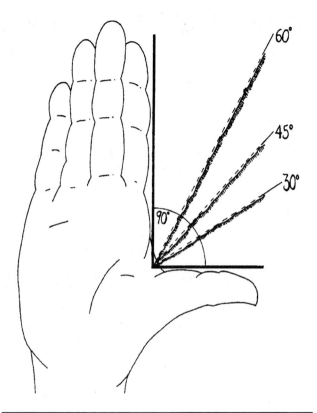

1.1.5. Estimating slope From The Map

The slope angle may also be estimated directly from the map as
follows:

Slope Angle	No of thick contours in 1 cm of map 1:50 000	1:25 000	Remarks
10°	2	1	Walking up a steep hill
20°	3.5	1.8	Steep, take care
30°	6	3	Zig Zag up, straight down
40°	8	4	Max angle of scree slopes
50°	12	6	Near limit if friction on rock
60°	16	8	Extremely steep

1.1.6. Naismith's Calculation For Speed

Naismith devised this basic equation to allow simplified planning.

- Determine the total length of your intended route.
- Work out the total height to be climbed.

The basic calculation devised by Naismith is;

5 km per hour, 1 Km in 12 mins or 100m in 1 min 12 secs
plus 30 mins for each 300m of ascent, 1 minute per
10 meters.

Naismith suggested two modifications

- Going gently down hill deduct 10 mins per 300m of descent.
- Going steeply down hill add 10 mins per 300m of descent.

1.1.7. Naismith Modified

The following equations should be used conservatively. They are designed to take into consideration composition of a group by compensating for the variety of fitness and experience levels.

- For a group of mixed ability adults use, 4 kph plus 1 hour for each 450m of ascent.
- For groups of mixed ability children (Adult leaders) use, 3 kph plus 1hr for each 300m of ascent.

1.1.8. Your Contact & Route Card

Your contact should know where you are going, when you plan to be back and what equipment you are carrying. This person must be reliable and take appropriate steps if you fail to reach your destination. i.e. a parent or partner, or the reception in your hotel or hostel. You must inform this contact when you complete your route and that you are all safe.

If you can, photocopy the section of map that you are using and draw your intended route onto it. NB, Ordnance Survey and other maps are protected by copyright. If not, leave a copy of annex F.

1.2. Weather Planning

1.2.0. Introduction

The aim of this section is to highlight some weather factors which you may find useful whilst on the move. Invariably they are all subject to local variation. All are applicable anywhere in the UK and Ireland although specific examples have been used, i.e. wind storms in the Cairngorm.

With a little planning it may be possible to get a good day out in what otherwise might be a miserable day. This section looks at weather and where to get information.

In general mountain weather tends to be substantially windier, wetter and colder than the surrounding lowland areas.

1.2.1. Lapse Rate (change of temperature with altitude)

As a rough guide, as you **gain altitude** ambient air temperature drops by;

- Dry air (hot or cold bright day) 1°C per 100m.
- Wet air (cloudy, foggy or humid) 1°C per 200m.

In the UK for planning purposes, if it is not obviously very wet or very dry, use 1°C per 150m of ascent.

As a rough guide, as you **loose altitude** ambient air temperature increases by 1°C per 100m.

The exception to the rule is when there is an inversion. The temperature in the low ground is cold and as you gain altitude the air gets warmer. If you are really lucky you may break through the cloud to find a magnificent view where everything except the mountain tops is swathed in cloud.

1.2.2. Beaufort Scale - Wind Speed

The Beaufort scale is a user friendly method of determining wind speed and strength by observing the effect of the wind on natural objects such as water and trees.

Scale	Described As	Speed kph	Effect
0	Calm	0	Smoke rises vertically
1	Light Air	3-6	Smoke and loose snow may drift a little
2	Light Breeze	7-12	Leaves rustle
3	Gentle Breeze	13-19	Leaves, rushes & grass move. Flags extended
4	Moderate	20-29	Raises dust & paper
5	Fresh	30-39	Crested wavelets on lakes, small trees sway
6	Strong	40-50	Large waves and spray on lakes. Wind whistles in crags
7	Moderate Gale	51 -61	Difficult to walk against the wind. Risk of frost nip on exposed flesh
8	Gale	62-74	Very hard walking, energy output doubled. Shroud of blowing snow up to 50m high
9	Strong Gale	75-87	Almost impossible to walk. Some damage to buildings. Streams blown back. Trailing ropes will be horizontal off the ground
10	Storm	88-101	Difficulty standing. Safer on hands & knees. Seek shelter. Energy output trebled. Whirlwinds of blowing snow on crests, plumes and streamers.
11	Violent Storm	102-131	Impossible to stand. Widespread damage. Spindrift forms a suspended shroud up to 100m high. Exposed flesh freezes
12	Hurricane	132+	Disaster everywhere. wind may lift and carry you across the ground. Breathing difficult when facing into wind

1.2.3. Wind Chill Factor

Wind chill factor is a measure of how much colder moving air is from still air, i.e. if the air temperature behind a building is 10°C the air temperature in the open with the wind blowing at force 3 (13 - 19 kph) is down to just 5°C. It is of great importance to understand the effect of the wind on air temperature.

Wind Speed

Force	Kmph	Ambient Air Temperature °C				
0	0	5	0	-5	-10	-15
1	1 - 6	-2	-6	-11	-16	-21
2	7 - 12	-3	-7	-12	-18	-22
3	13 - 19	-6	-10	-15	-21	-26
4	20 - 29	-8	-14	-18	-24	-30
5	30 - 39	-18	-23	-30	-36	-42
6	40 - 49	-24	-31	-38	-44	-50
7	50 - 59	-52	-58	-64	-70	-73

°C	Remarks
1 to 4	Cool
-10 to 0	Cold
-20 to -11	Very cold
-30 to -21	Bitterly cold. Little danger if properly clothed
-40 to -31	Considerable danger, exposed flesh freezes
-50 to -41	Very grave danger, exposed flesh freezes within 1 minute

1.2.4. Thunder & Lightning - Flash to Bang

Mountain tops and ridges can be very dangerous places during thunder storms. To avoid unnecessary worry try to work out if the storm is coming towards you or going away from you.

- Sound travels at 330 m per second or 1 km in 3 seconds.
- Light travels at 300,000 km per sec.
- You will always observe lightning before you hear thunder.

To calculate how far away the storm is;
- Start counting as soon as you see the lightning flash.
- Stop counting as soon as you here the thunder.

Seconds are accurately counted by counting as one thousand and one, one thousand and two and so on.

- Divide the number of seconds by 3.
- This equals the distance from the storm in km.

For example, if you counted 12 seconds. 12 ÷ 3 = 4.
Therefore the thunder storm is 4 km away.

Repeat this for subsequent lightening flashes.

Flash to bang time is **decreasing** - the storm is **coming closer**.
Flash to bang time is **increasing** - the storm is **moving away.**

1.2.5. Wind Storms

An important consideration for route planning, especially in the winter months is that wind speeds are greatly increased over hills that face in a southerly direction.

This is especially so when there are strong South Easterly winds and a stable upper atmosphere. Gentler winds at lower altitudes are forced over mountain tops increasing their speed enormously. These are known as orographic winds.

As the wind clears the mountain tops and ridge the sudden release of pressure forces the wind down into corries and cwms where they circulate vigorously forcing spindrift, rain and other debris up the steep back walls and back onto the ridgeline or mountain top.

During the winter months these devastating wind storms may dominate for many days. Average monthly wind speeds vary between 56 kph and 88 kph and they can easily pick up fully equipped mountaineers and throw them many meters. Wind speeds can change very rapidly to the extent that progress can only be made by crawling along the ground.

The windiest month tends to be March. Gusts up to 275 kph have been recorded in Cairngorm.

Ridge walks are probably best avoided during these periods, although progress can be made provided you stay off the crest or away from the top of steep slopes and cliffs.

1.3. Information

1.3.0. Introduction

All weather information should be analysed and applied to the
terrain you are in, i.e. the weather forecast for Bangor North
Wales will be nothing like the conditions 10 miles inland in
Snowdonia.

1.3.1. Where To Get Weather Information

TV forecasts give general area forecasts and are not to be relied
upon for mountain areas. Newspaper bulletins are not up to date.
Broadsheets tend to give a better indication of what is going on,
they also give sun rise and set, moon state and tide tables. Some
local papers may give better forecasts than the national papers.
Telephone, local and national radio forecasts are covered below.

1.3.2. Telephone Forecasts

The Met Office (www.metoffice.com)

Mountain Area Forecasts by Phone. For local weather
forecasts in mountainous areas call **09068 500** followed by; **441**
Highlands West. **442** Highlands East. **449** Snowdonia. **484**
Lakes.

Premium Rate Fax. Call **09060 100** followed by **405** Highlands
West. **406** Highlands East. **407** Lakes. **408** Snowdonia.

Climbline (Newstel Ltd.) Gives detailed reports for a number
of areas in UK mountainous regions - wind speed and direction,
cloud base, freezing level and, in winter, avalanche reports.
09001 654669

Weather Check - UK general forecasts are available on **09001
654661**

1.3.3. Radio Stations

The best radio forecast comes from the Shipping Forecast on Radio 4 and is described below. For all other radio stations bear in mind that frequencies are approximate in the regions indicated, so try several frequencies to get the best reception.

It is best to scan your radio dial to find a workable frequency for the area that you are in. Experience suggests that these forecasts are aimed at the populated areas of each region and are limited in scope. The following stations may be useful.

- Moray Firth Radio. Inverness   97.4 Mhz & 1107 Khz
- Nevis Radio.   Fort William 96.6 Mhz
- BBC Scotland.   Inverness   94.0 Mhz

For best FM reception position the radio at different places, usually as high as possible. Try the antenna at different angles including vertically and orientate the radio to get the strongest signal.

For AM (Medium Wave) band, many radios are still calibrated in wavelengths. To convert frequency to wave length divide 300,000 by the frequency in kHz eg 300,000 ÷ 1215 kHz 247 meters. AM and FM frequencies are restricted by mountains, nearby buildings and even trees.

Medium wave is normally received on an internal antenna in your radio, position the radio high and orientate it to get the best reception. At night this is more important as there will be a lot of interference from stations on nearby frequencies. TVs and other electrical devices also produce a lot of interference. Reorientate the radio for each frequency, frequency may drift so realign the radio as this starts to happen.

1.3.4. Radio 4 - The Shipping Forecast

This section allows you to gather the latest weather information direct from the BBC Shipping Forecast, to plot it on the maps provided and to assist you in making reasonable deductions about what is likely to happen in the coming hours.

Forecasts in sea areas apply to adjacent mountain areas at 610m (2000 ft). Like all forecasts the information is to be interpreted and applied to the appropriate region. The synopsis at the begining of the forecast gives a good overall picture.

The Met Office/Royal Yachting Association produce pads of A4 size Met Maps for logging the Shipping Forecast. See useful addresses.

1.3.5. Radio 4 Timings

BBC Shipping Forecast. Radio 4
FM 92.4 - 94.6Mhz. LW 198Khz (1515m)

Shipping Forecast at 0048, 0555 (LW), 1355, 1750.

The Shipping Forecast is brief, comprehensive and issued at dictation speed it takes 5 minutes flat. The content is:

Gale warnings in operation. The forecast for the next 24 hours (Wind, weather and visibility). General synopsis of where the Highs and Lows are and which way they are moving. A selection of up-to-date reports from coastal stations.

1.3.6. Using The Shipping Forecast

- Note the time of the report. Move everything on accordingly.
- Use all the available information and draw a UK wide map. It will help you visualise what is going on.
- Wind is always stated as the direction IT IS COMING FROM.

Wind speed is normally issued in knots. The knot is a measure of time and distance.
- 1 Knot 1.15 Mph and 20 knots 23Mph.
- 1 Knot 1.85 Kmph and 20 knots 37Kmh.

Visibility is given in nautical miles (nm).
- To convert nm to miles x 1.15 and nm to Km   x 1.85.
- To convert miles to nm x 0.87 and miles to Km x 1.61.
- To convert Km to nm   x 0.72 and Km to miles x 0.63.

1.3.7. Definitions Used

Speed of Systems
- Slowly   up to 15 knots (27.25 kph).
- Steadily   1.5-2.5 knots (up to 46.25 kph).
- Rather quickly 25-35 knots (up to 64.85 kph).
- Rapidly   35-45 knots (up to 83.25 kph).
- Very rapidly   Over 45 knots (over 83.25 kph).

Visibility
- Fog   less than 1000m visibility.
- Poor   1000m to 2nm (3700 m) visibility.
- Moderate 2-5nm (3700-9250 m) visibility.
- Good   Over 5nm (Over 9250 m) visibility.

Pressure change
- Steady   Less than 0.1 mb in past 3 hrs.
- Rising/falling slowly   0.1-1.5 mb in past 3 hrs.
- Rising/falling   1.6-3.5 mb in past 3 hrs.
- Rising/falling quickly   3.5-6 mb in past 3 hrs.
- Rising/falling very rapidly Over 6 mb in past 6 hrs.

Gale Warnings - Gale due to start
- **Imminent** Within 6 hours of warning time.
- **Soon**   Within 6-12 hours of warning time.
- **Later**   More than 12 hours from warning time.

Warning time - the time stated as "Gale warning as at 1500BST" in the forecast.

Practice taking forecasts and plotting information before you venture out into the mountains.

Sumburgh

3

Butt of Lewis

2

Tiree

1

Fifeness

4

Malin Head

13

Smiths
Knoll
Auto

Ronaldsway

12

5

Valentia

11

Dover

6

7

Royal Sovereign

Lands End

10

9

Channel Light Vessel

Jersey

8

| 0 | 100 | 200 | 300 Nautical Miles |

| 0 | 200 | 400 | 600 | 800 Km |

17

Lerwick 17

Stornoway 16 18 Wick

Benbecula 15 19 Aberdeen

14. Prestwick
13. Corsewell Point
12. Larne 20 Leuchars
11. Orloch Head
10. Killoch 1 Boulmer

14

12 13 Bridlington

11 2

10

9 8

Ronaldsway

Valley 7 Blackpool

Walton on
the Naze

6 Mumbles 3

Lands End 5 4

St Catherines
Point

0 100 200 300 Nautical Miles

0 200 400 600 800 Km

1.4. Food, Drink & Energy

1.4.0. Introduction

A fit body requires a balance between calorific intake and energy output. This varies between individuals, depending on physical activity, height, weight, sex, age, rate of metabolism, hormonal activity and emotional state.

To get the best from yourself on a day in the mountains calculate how many calories you will need. This information is for guidance only. There are many texts available which deal with all the nutrients required.

1.4.1. Energy Input

Carbohydrates should make up 60% of daily kcal intake. There are 4 kcal in 1g of carbohydrate. These are the primary source of energy because the body can break them down easily.

Protein should make up 15% of daily kcal intake. They are needed for amino acids which are used by the body for structure and function. There are 4 kcal in 1g of protein. Proteins are less readily broken down by the body than carbohydrates.

Fats should make up to 25% of daily kcal intake or 35% in colder climates. There are 9 kcal in 1g of fat. In winter add more fats to your diet, they play an important role in bodily function, energy reserves and insulation. Fat is a concentrated form of fuel which is released slowly. It is also used during normal metabolic function.

Typical intake for a normal day's activity of 3000 Kcals

- Carbohydrates   60%   1800 kcal
- Protein   up to 15%   450 kcal
- Fats   up to 25%   750 kcal

An interesting fact is that you will invariably develop a profound dislike for fats at altitudes over 4572 m (15000 ft). Carbohydrate intake increases to compensate with up to 3 times the normal amount consumed in sweet drinks.

1.4.2. Energy Output

The average adult in good physical condition can sustain output of up to 630 kcal per hour for short periods of time. Below are some typical output values.

	kcal per min	per hour
Sleep	1	60
Sitting Writing	2	120
Walking 2 mph hard ground	3	180
Walking 2 mph 1:4 incline	11	660
Walking 2.5 mph on grass	6	360
Walking 2.5 mph on soft snow	14	840
Climbing 1:6 with 10 kg load	12	720
Climbing 1:4 with 10 kg load	13	780
Running cross country	11	660
Skiing 4 mph level hard snow	10	600
Canoeing 4 mph	7	420
Cycling 10 mph	7	420
Mountain Biking 10 mph	10	600
Driving a car	3	180
Swimming 25 meters per min	7	420
Base metabolic rate		70
Base metabolic rate		1700 per day
Normal days work		3000 per day
Winter camping expeditions		3700 to 4200 per day

1.4.3. Planned Kcal Expenditure

If you are planning a 25 km walk with an expected total height gain of 1000 m. From the chart below;

- Read along the bottom line to the 25 km point.
- Now read up the column until you meet the 1000 m line.
- Read off the kcal expenditure column on the left.

In this case the planned expenditure is approximately 4300 kcals.

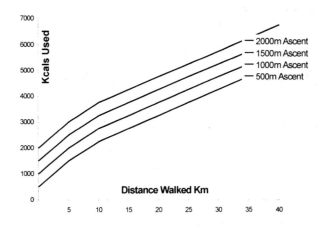

1.4.4. Water Requirements

Human body temperature depends on the balance between heat production by metabolism and from the environment against heat losses to the environment by breathing, sweating and excretion. The body is able to regulate temperature by a complex interaction between the liver and kidneys, the other organs and the skin.

Loss of water causes metabolism to slow down, thermal regulation is inhibited and the effects of dehydration set in, the casualty soon goes into a state of collapse by over heating.

- 1 to 5% loss of body weight due to dehydration causes thirst, discomfort and nausea.
- 6 to 10% loss of body weight due to dehydration causes dizziness, headache, loss of salivation, tingling in the limbs, reduced urine production and as the condition worsens, cyanosis (blue tinge of the skin).

Yellow orange urine indicates dehydration, the darker the colour the more serious the problem.

Average daily water requirements are;

Input. Minimum daily requirement is 2.6 litres.
Output. The average daily output is 2.6 litres.

Input	mls	Output	mls
Ingested as solids	850	Urine	1500
Ingested as liquid	1400	Faeces	200
Metabolism	350	Breathing & Sweating	900
Totals	**2600**		**2600**

Metabolism produces water as a waste product which is dealt with by the liver and kidneys.

In cold conditions more moisture is lost in the breath.
In hot conditions more moisture is lost by sweating.

Liquids must be replaced regularly throughout the day. Thirst lags behind actual water requirement. You must anticipate fluid loss and take more water before the onset of thirst occurs.

The thirst quenching effect of cold liquid induces a craving for it. Put simply, the colder the liquid the more your body will want. The average body always reacts to eject cold liquids from the stomach so there is a net loss of heat. So, always give warm fluids to casualties, especialy to those with cold injuries.

The balance between dehydration and heat loss in the victim should be carefully considered. Dehydration will cause greater concern than the heat loss.

- **1 litre of water at 55°C** provides 18 kcal of energy.
- **1 litre of water at 1°C** uses 37 kcals to reach normal core temperature.

1.4.5. Energy Loss At Rest

Energy is required to maintain bodily functions when at rest or sleeping. The amount of energy used depends on the temperature, the figures below show that less energy is used if the body is kept warm.

Temperature °C	kcals per hour used
20	6
0	13
-4	19
-40	26

1.4.6. Kcal Losses in Wind

This table is derived from Steadman's experiments on windchill in 1971. These were conducted at an ambient air temperature of 0°C.

The subject was wearing a layered clothing system and expenditure is in kcals per hour. The table gives the number of kcals needed by the body to sustain a constant 4.8 kph walking speed and maintain body warmth.

Wind Speed	Dry Base Layer	Wet Base Layer	Naked
nil	450-530	550-630	650-750
32kph (Force 5)	750-850	1030-1130	1300-1400
64kph (Force 8)	1000-1100	1400-1500	2000-2100

Base layers may become wet by sweating, water encroaching through cuffs, ankles and neckline. The table is an indication of expenditure, it would take a supremely fit athlete to maintain the work output indicated above.

1.4.7. The Shivering Response

Shivering is the body's attempt to produce heat . If the body is entering the hypothermic state there will be a consequential 25% increase in lost heat. The body works hard to counter the effects of the cold and wet. This rapid heat loss must be stopped.

Reduce losses by protecting the casualty from the ground and covering them with dry and waterproof garments. The heat produced by the shivering response will then benefit the casualty. If the casualty is able, feed them sweet warm drinks and give them a high calorie snack, this quickly replaces lost Kcals and feeds the body's demand for more heat.

1.4.8. Sweating & Wet Clothing

The body regulates heat by sweating and increased breathing rate. At rest this sweat begins to evaporate causing cooling.

- In warmer weather this is a beneficial effect.

- In cold weather cooling causes the body to feel cold. To prevent this cooling the body and base layer garments must be kept dry.

This is achieved by increasing ventilation during work, by opening zips and removing hats, gloves and excess garments. At rest they are all closed up again and warmth is retained.

Wet clothing may hold over ½kg of water. It takes 245 Kcals to heat that water up. The heat losses induced by wet clothing are potentially very serious.

1.4.9 Bodily Waste

More and more people are going to the hills every year and human waste is becoming a problem because everyone needs to "Go" at some stage or other.

It often seems that people don't care because they just "go" wherever and whenever they please. The effect is the stench of stale urine and unsightly toilet paper sticking out from behind rocks.

This practice is unhygenic and unacceptable. The issue is already at crisis levels in most national parks in the USA, where back packers have to carry solid waste away with them.

In the interests of the environment and public health, it is strongly recommended that all mountain users carry enough plastic bags into which all solid bodily waste matter can be placed for safe disposal.

Urine.

- Go a minimum of 50 meters from any water course, do not do it in the middle of the path or track.
- In wild campsites mark the location of the loo so that everyone uses the same place. In winter this is even more important as you may need snow as a source of fresh water.

Defecation.

- Always carry enough plastic bags to cope with each personal hygene event.

The whole package tends to be heavy, soft and prone to burst if mal-treated. Stow carefully in your rucksack in a place where there is the least possible risk of bursting.

If you genuinely must defecate on the ground then follow these simple guidelines;

- Go well away from any water course, right of way or place where others may wish to pitch a tent or stop for a picnic.
- Dig a hole with a trowel to a depth of at least 30 cm.
- Ensure that all your doings and the paper go in the hole then replace all the soil on top.
- In winter, dig through the snow to the solid ground then dig a small hole as above otherwise your mess will reappear when the snow melts. Only then will it begin to smell and ruin the countryside.

Other Waste Material

Sanitary towels and soiled disposable nappies must be bagged up and taken off the mountain in a similar way as feaces.

2. Navigation

2.0. Introduction

Being able to navigate in all weather conditions and at night will reduce the chances of becoming lost. Yet many people believe that navigation is something for others to do, something which is all too difficult. This could not be further from the truth.

With a few simple skills and plenty of practice navigation can be an absolute joy. Practicing the skills is not difficult as there are more and more fixed orienteering courses being set up all round the country. Most are designed by experienced navigators to incorporate the skills and techniques described in this section. They are relatively safe places to practice navigation and route finding skills.

Basics such as what a map is or how to use a compass, are not covered here, but they are in Langmuir E (1995) Mountaincraft And Leadership, and other books. See 7.5. References and further reading.

2.1. Basics

2.1.0. Global Positioning Systems (GPS)

These have not been considered here because most people will probably never have access to one. Without a doubt GPS is a revolutionary step forward in navigation. But we must all be able to find our way by the basic techniques and methods just in case the GPS fails. Treat GPS as a bonus to be enjoyed but not relied upon.

2.1.1. The Mark One Eye Ball

The mark one eye ball is the most important item of navigation equipment. It normally comes in pairs mounted at the front of the head. This enables us to see where we are going with a clear field of vision. But the eyes are susceptible to bright light, cold rain and wind, blizzards and prolonged exposure to narrow beams of torch light.

In winter carry a pair of ski goggles to protect your eyes. This will enable you to read the map and compass without squinting through ice encrusted eye lashes. In summer consider using sunglasses which filter out ultra violet (UV) light.

2.1.2. Torch Light - (SITO) Switch It Off

Good navigation at night and in bad weather is dependant on being able to make out the ground in front of you. As a rule use your torch only for checking the map and setting the compass, then **S**witch **IT O**ff.

The essence of night vision is that you can perceive a range of ground in front of you. Torch light focuses vision down the beam so that most features either side are missed. Your range of vision and navigation skills become restricted too. Keep one eye closed to preserve night vision when checking your map by torch light.

2.2. The Map

2.2.0. The Map

The map is probably the second most important navigational tool. You can navigate very satisfactorily with just the map under most conditions. Give some consideration to how you look after and use your maps.

Mine are cut to remove the protective card only. They are protected using clear sticky back plastic. This enables me to fold the map to fit in my pockets or in my hand when I'm thumbing in poor weather.

Ready laminated maps are available for many parts of the UK.

2.2.1. Holding The Map

Holding the map so it is facing the way you are going will aid your navigation. For instance, if you are walking in a southerly direction then hold it as shown below. This is also known as setting the map. In this way what you see in front of you is what you see on the map. There is reduced risk of confusion and what is a right turn on the map is a right turn on the ground.

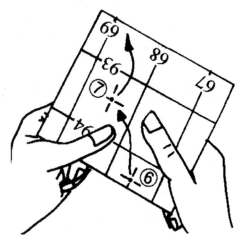

2.2.2. Thumbing

Thumbing is a bad weather technique but requires that the map be folded in such a way that it fits in your hand comfortably. The thumb is kept on the point where you are and is moved as you pass recognisable features. This use of the map coupled with timing and pacing focuses the mind specifically on keeping direction and finding your way.

Notice that the user has a route going from north to south so is holding the map upside down. South on the map is facing south on the ground. The map is folded to fit in one hand.

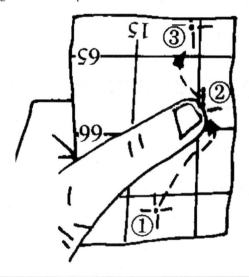

2.2.3. Marking The Map

There are three important ways in which you can mark your maps. Each is designed to help you read the map more easily.

The first is to take a highlighter pen and mark all the eastings and northings. Most 1:50 000 Ordnance Survey maps now have these numbers on the main body of the map as well as at the margin.

Most Ordnance Survey maps have contours drawn so that each 5th contour is thicker than the ones in between, these are known as index contours. To make them stand out even more and thus aid your perception of altitude, take a 2B pencil and carefully draw over each index contour. This has the added bonus of emphasising the shape of the terrain too.

Thirdly. mark your route directly onto the map. If you decide to do this a good option is to cover the map with clear sticky back plastic first. Mark the map with a very fine over head projector (OHP) permanent marker. This ensures that your route is not washed off in the rain but can be rubbed off using a plastic eraser.

2.2.4. Tick Off Features

Each section of your route is called a leg. Each leg is between two easily identifiable features on the map which are also seen on the ground. To aid navigation each leg should be no longer than 250 to 300 meters, or up to 1000 meters in open ground.

As you pass each feature tick it off in your mind or on your map, you can now see quickly and clearly where you have been and roughly how long ago you were there.

This example is derived from an area in grid square NN45 88 on the OS Landranger sheet 42 of Glen Garry and Loch Rannoch. The spur is Sròn á Ghoire (Nose of the Corrie) on Creag Meagaidh National Nature Reserve.

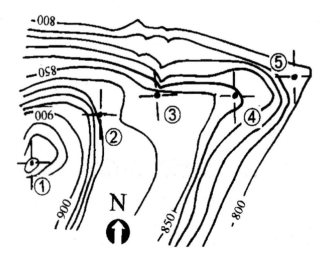

The route is, ① North East from top of rounded hill top to ②
bottom of steep slope. Then cross flatter terrain to ③ top of steep
slope. Follow in an easterly direction to ④ prominent spur, then
down hill to ⑤, an area of flatter terrain on the spur.

2.2.5. Handrail Features

These are features on the ground that you can use to guide you
along your route i.e. from ③ to ④ on the sketch above. Other
features such as a ridge line, a stream or a boundary wall or fence
can be used.

- From ① pace North West to the boundry (wall or fence) at ②.
- ② is also at the bottom of a steep slope, and at a change in
  direction of the boundary. Follow this handrail feature North
  to where the ground becomes markedly steeper at ③.
- From ③ pace East along the bottom of this handrail slope then
  take a bearing south to the target at ④.

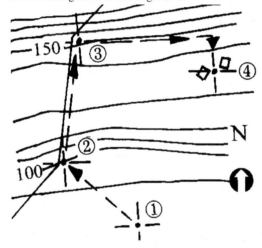

2.2.6. Cut Off Features

These are obvious features which, if you reach them, you know
you have gone too far i.e. a track, ground starts going down hill, a
stream or a wood line. If you reach the cut off feature you should
be able to pace back along your bearing to your intended target.

2.3. Direction

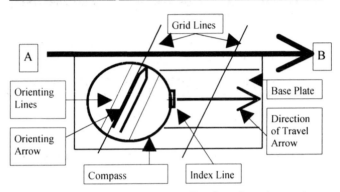

1. Lay your compass on the map, the direction of travel arrow is aligned along the direction you wish to travel i.e. from A to B.
2. Rotate the compass housing until the orienting lines and the orienting arrow line up with the grid lines. Check that the orienting arrow is pointing North i.e. at the top of the map.
3. Read the bearing displayed at the index line.
4. Make your magnetic correction (see below)
5. To travel in the right direction, hold the compass flat with the direction of travel arrow pointing away from yourself. Turn your whole body until the North needle lines up with the Orienting arrow.
6. Your are traveling to where the direction of arrow is pointing. As you proceed check that the North needle is aligned under the Orienting arrow.

Trust Your Compass

2.3.1. Compass Corrections

There are two ways to get a compass bearing. Directly from the map or by pointing your compass at an object or feature on the ground. In doing so remember that a correction for magnetic variation has to be made.

GRID refers to a grid bearing taken from the map. **MAG** refers to magnetic bearing taken from or to a feature on the ground. To help you remember how to apply magnetic variation try this little ditty;

GRID to MAG : ADD. Add the number of degrees of magnetic variation to your compass. OR

MAG to GRID : GET RID. Subtract the number of degrees of magnetic variation from your compass.

2.3.2. Position Finding - Aspect Of Slope

If you suspect that you are temporarily lost then one way to help you decide where you are is to work out the aspect of the slope.

Take a bearing either directly down or up the hill at right angles to the contours.

This bearing (don't forget mag to grid get rid) is the aspect of the slope. You may need to employ other techniques to enable you to be reasonably certain that you are where you think you are.

This examples below illustrates the different slope aspects on similar compass bearings in a 1 Km grid square NN18 72 on the OS Landranger sheet 41 of Ben Nevis. The col is between Carn Mor Dearg and Aonach Mor.

- If the aspect of slope is downhill 270° (due West) then you must be on ridge line ①. The slopes either side of you will also be dropping away sharply.

- If the aspect is downhill 90° (Due East) then you must be on ridge line ②. The slopes either side of you will also be dropping away sharply.

- If the slope aspect is downhill 225° (South West), then you must be standing somewhere on the slope ③.

- But if the slope is uphill 225° (South West), then you must be standing somewhere on the slope ④.

This method can also be used when contouring, for example;

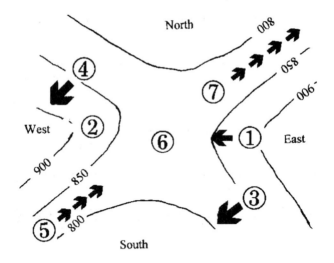

- If you have a bearing of 45° (North East) and you are contouring with high ground to your left then you must be on the slope ⑤. To pin point your position more accurately continue on this bearing for a little longer until you reach the col ⑥ or the ridge ②.

- If you have a bearing of 45° (North East) and you are contouring with high ground to your right then you must be on the slope ⑦.

- If the ground is flatish but dropping away to the North and South you must be on the col ⑥ but confirm this by checking that the ground rises to the East and West.

2.3.3. Drift

Drift is when you are deflected from your planned course by;

- A natural bias to drift either left or right when walking on a compass bearing.

- A tendancy to drift down hill when contouring.

- Deflection off course caused by strong winds or rain and snow coming from one side.

The magnitude of the drift depends on the accuracy of your map and compass work and what steps you take to compensate. The easiest way to compensate is to assess the factor causing you to drift and then deliberately aim off. For instance;

- If a strong wind is causing you to drift to the left of your bearing then force yourself to walk right of the bearing.

- If you are contouring round a hill then deliberately force yourself to walk slightly up hill.

2.3.4. Finding Direction Using The Sun

To find East and West;

- Place a stick in the ground.
- Mark the end of the shadow.
- Wait 10 to 15 minutes.
- Mark the end of the subsequent shadow.
- Draw a line between the two.
- The first marker drawn is West.
- The second marker drawn is East.

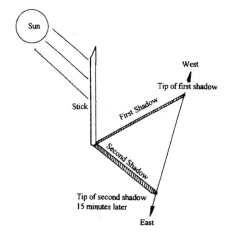

To find south using a watch (Northern hemisphere);

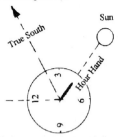

- Point the hour hand of your watch at the sun.
- South is the point half way between the hour hand and 12 on your watch face.

2.3.5. Keeping Direction

Keeping direction during daylight may pose a few problems. Perhaps the easiest way to achieve this is to look in the general direction that you are travelling and divide the ground into near, middle and far. Choose immovable features which should be obvious even if the weather or daylight begin to deteriorate.

The example below is the view South West from Cairngorm summit at 1245 m. The weather monitoring station is immediately behind the viewer.

First, look into the far distance. ① is Carn Toul 1291m, ② is Angel Peak 1258 m and ③ is Braeriach 1296 m. They are all about 8 Km away. The deep gorge of Lairig Ghru is hidden from view between the observer and these three peaks.

212° Grid   218° Grid   233° Grid

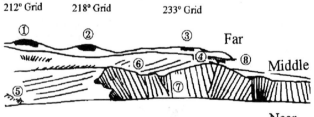

Next look into the middle distance. ④ is Cairn Lochan 1215 m, about 2.5 mm away. ⑤ is Coire Raibeirt 1 km away and ⑥ Coire Domhain about 1.5 km away. These are all part of the high Cairngorm plateau. To the West are the steep cliffs of Coire an t sneachda ⑦ 750 m away and Coire Lochan ⑧ 2.5 km away.

In the near ground, all around is the boulder field of Cairngorm summit, the field of view is about 350 m.

The essence of having these essential features in the mind is that there is great danger to the right of our field of view and in the far distance below the far horizon.

As weather deteriorates or light begins to fail focus on the closer ground, take bearings before vision is lost altogether and be aware of the dangers all around.

2.3.6. Keeping Direction - Night

The art of keeping direction at night is based on minimising the use of the torch. Use the torch to check the map and take a bearing then switch it off, wait for about 30 seconds and your eyes adjust to open up a whole new world. Even in what is apparently total darkness you will be able to make out the difference between the sky and the ground. If the moon or stars are out you may even be able to make out features in the landscape.

Because your eyes are now adjusted they have a full range of view and you will be able to determine the horizon. Face the direction that you are going in and pick out a shape on the horizon that you can use either to aim at directly or which you can aim off left or right of. You must use this technique in conjunction with timing and pacing. You will be suprised at just how accurate you can be.

2.3.7. Keeping Direction - Winter

The biggest problem in winter both during the day and at night is that everything is covered in snow. The appearance of the ground changes completely from what is shown on the map. Secondly, everything is white meaning that you can not pick out features on the ground to aim at. Trust your compass and always use timing and pacing. At the very least your mind will be focused on direction, distance travelled and time.

2.4. Distance

Knowing how long it takes to walk a given distance on a variety of terrain is an essential navigation tool. The table below gives the average time taken to cover given distances by an averagely fit person carrying a small rucksack.

Timings (Based on Naismith at 5 Kph)
Minutes : Seconds

Distance walked (meters)	50	100	150	500	1000
Hard level surface	0:36	1:12	1:48	6:00	12:0
Variable, undulating	0:45	1:30	2:15	7:30	15:0
Firm Snow	1:00	2:00	3:00	10:0	20:0
Deep snow, steep slope	1:30	3:00	4:30	15:0	30:0

Example. Walking 150 m on firm snow should take 3 minutes for the average person. It would take 4.5 minutes to walk the same distance in deep snow.

If you know that you can walk 100 meters in 3 minutes in deep snow and you have 500 meters of ground to cover to your next tick off feature, then it should take 15 minutes to cover that ground.

If after 20 minutes you have not reached the next tick off feature, then stop and check that you are still on course. If you are on course then walk on for another 10% of the original plan time i.e. 1.5 minutes. If you are off course then consider returning to your last known position and start again.

You may ask yourself, am I walking as fast as I normally do? This depends on the nature of the ground or on how tired you are. If you are going slower then continue walking for a few more minutes to compensate.

2.4.1. Pacing

Pacing is an essential navigational tool. It is important that you know what your personal pacings are. The length of your stride is modified by the nature of the ground, i.e. how steep it is, is it wet or dry, firm or boggy and importantly is this the start of an invigorating day or the end of a very cold and wet one?.

One complete pace is counted each time the left foot strikes the ground. (Right if you prefer.)

The table below gives the number of paces an average sized, averagely fit person takes carrying a small rucksack.

Distance (Meters)	50	100	150	500	1000
Hard level surface	30	59	88	295	590
Variable, undulating	42	71	106	354	708
Firm Snow	47	94	142	472	944
Deep snow, steep slope	59	118	177	590	1188

Example. The average person takes 59 paces to cover 100 m on a hard level surface.

We know that we can walk 100 meters in 59 double paces. So, if the next leg is 500 meters then we know that the minimum number of paces is going to be 5 x 59   295 paces.

If we walk along our route for 500 paces then we know for certain that we have over shot the mark and we should retrace our steps to find the target. If we have walked only 270 paces then we know that we can not possibly have reached the target so we must press on a little further.

Timing and pacing form the basis of a double check on our navigation by suggesting that within a certain time and within a cetain number of paces we will reach the target.

These timing and pacing tables are for guidance only. Work out your own pace and timings on flat terrain over an accurately measured 100m carrying a mid weight rucksack. Then try it out on the terrain indicated. There are blank tables at annex C for you to adapt for personal use.

2.4.2. Distances To The Horizon

Knowing how far you can see in daylight is an aid to navigation. The table below gives some approximate distances for a range of altitudes. A crude measure to use is the square root of the altitude in meters + $^1/_3$ of that. Now multiply the sum by 3 = km to the horizon. All distances and altitudes are rounded to the nearest whole number. Refraction is taken into account.

Altitude Meters	Square root of a	1/3rd of b	Sum of b + c	Multiply d by 3 = Horizon	Remarks
a	b	c	d		
1.8	1.35	0.45	1.8	**5 km**	
10	3.16	1.1	4.26	**13 km**	
50	7.1	2.4	9.5	**29 km**	
100	10	3.3	13.3	**40 km**	
500	22.4	7.5	29.9	**90 km**	
839	29	9.7	38.7	**116 km**	Mourne Mts
962	31	10.3	41.3	**124 km**	Scafell Pike
1000	31.6	10.5	42.1	**126 km**	
1085	33	11	44	**132 km**	Snowdon
1364	37	12.3	49.3	**148 km**	Ben Nevis

2.4.3. Map Grid Squares

Judging distance from the popular outdoor maps in UK is simple because each grid square = 1km.

- **1:50 000 maps** 1 km = 2 cm (2 mm = 100 m, 1 cm = 500 m). The distance diagonally across the grid square is (2.8 cm) = 1.4 km.
- **1:25 000 maps** 1 km = 4 cm (2 mm = 50 m, 4 mm = 100 m, 1cm = 250 m, 2 cm = 500 m). The distance diagonally across the grid square is (5.6 cm) = 1.4 km

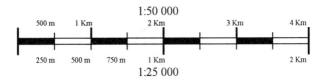

3. Hazardous Terrain

3.0. Introduction

Steep ground in summer and winter can be a daunting prospect for the walker. They can also be very exciting and beautiful places to be. To be comfortable on steep ground in all conditions will increase your confidence and that of your group. You may also venture to places which you would not have considered before.

This section also looks at the hazards associated with river crossings. Plan ahead to assess the probability of crossing rivers, what to consider if you are confronted with a raging torrent and what to do if there is no safer alternative to making a crossing. River crossings are potentially very dangerous and as a general rule should be avoided.

A cautionary note. Leaders of parties of walkers should only carry a rope for specific use in an emergency, i.e. for river crossings, making stretchers and for assistance over steep ground. If there is an expressed intention to use the rope then the leader must be suitably qualified.

3.1. Steep Ground Summer

3.1.0. Introduction

The only equipment carried to aid passage over difficult terrain is the rope. It is understood that the party is carrying the rope for emergency use only. Intent to use the rope indicates that the party is either climbing or scrambling or that the party is supervised by a suitably qualified person.

Walking parties should aim to avoid terrain where the rope will definitely be needed, aiming instead for suitably challenging routes which most of the group should be able to manage without too much fuss. It is better to keep the rope stowed away out of sight, otherwise people will expect you to use it. This may, in itself, cause some apprehension.

3.1.1. Security On Steep Ground

The leader must assess the party before proceding onto steeper terrain, if there is any doubt about anyone in the group then it is safer to stick to known paths.

There may be times when it is not possible to avoid steep ground. A sound principle for protecting the group is that the leader must always be below individuals to prevent them from going too far if they slip. Factors to consider as the party proceeds;

- **Difficulty.** Is a slip probable on this terrain?
- **Ability.** Individual reaction to exposure and difficulty?
- **Exposure.** Would a slip result in serious injury?
- **Security.** Can the situation be properly safe guarded with or without a rope?
- **Time.** Speed is often a safety factor in its own right. Is saving time more important than the additional security provided by roping up?
- **Margin Of Safety.** The party must be operating well within its experience and capabilities.

3.1.2. Protecting The Party

When ascending difficult terrain. The person leading the group is probably best positioned behind the weakest or most nervous person. The leader can protect this person for each little step physically.

In descent on difficult terrain. The leader should be at the front to protect each difficult section and to prevent the party wandering into possible danger. Stop the party and scout ahead as the ground dictates.

When traversing. The leader should be placed as dictated by the ground but should rest the party and scout ahead as necessary. Difficult sections should be protected by positioning yourself in such away that assistance can be given directly.

To protect difficult steps or traverses without using a rope the leader must be placed in such a way that the danger is covered, i.e. the leader may brace themselves and help everyone across a gap, or up and down difficult steps.

A hand placed securely on the nervous persons rucksack or against their shoulder blades will give them a great deal of confidence. The leader must ensure that if a fall or slip occurs they do not end up being a casualty. Never be afraid to retreat from difficult ground and work around it.

3.1.3. Roping Up

A 25 meter length of 9mm thickness rope should cover most situations. If you decide to use the rope ensure that it is used effectively and efficiently. Confidence roping should be actively avoided. The simplest use of the rope is as a dog lead.

3.1.4. The Dog Lead

This is used when the leader has concerns for a very nervous person on steep but walkable terrain. The principle is to have a very short, tight rope and the leader stays directly above the person. The leader may arrest movement by tugging the rope sharply to the ground forcing the other person to sit. As ever, best practice is to calm the person by talking to them continuously.

Spare rope tucked into rucksack

½ Meter Dog Lead

3.1.5. Selecting An Anchor

If the dog lead fails you may have to consider setting up a small belay. The most important part of the system is the anchor which you decide to use.

- Use the best anchor you can find. It must be bomb proof.
- Test the anchor thoroughly before using it. Avoid anything which moves.
- The anchor must be along the line of the belay.
- The anchor should not have sharp edges which could damage the rope. Otherwise use padding to protect the rope.
- The anchor must be big enough to prevent the rope from slipping off.

The Spike

The Thread

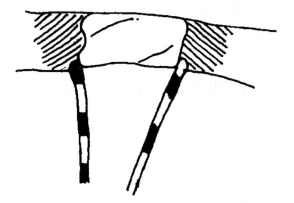

At this stage there is no need to attach the rope to either the rock or to yourself. Consider using the braced belay or the direct belay.

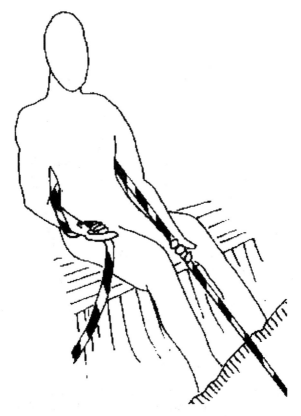

The belayer is the anchor and simply sits and braces against suitable ground. This sort of belay may be used for very short sections for 1 or 2 nervous people. The risk of a fall should be minimal. The belayer should be able to use the left or right arms equally.

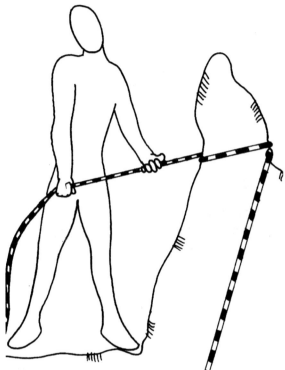

The anchor is more likely to be a spike. The rope is passed around the spike and the leader brings up the person controlling the rope with both hands. This method may be used for longer sections. Friction from the spike is sufficient to hold a fall. This method is very good for helping someone down steep sections too. Note that the term spike refers to any object which the rope can be passed around.

The question of indirect belays (those where the rope is tied to the rock and the belayer tied to the rope) is outside the scope of this book. But the principles of belaying are the same.

3.1.9. The Principles Of Belaying

- The rope between the belay, the belayer and the person being belayed must be as straight, and as tight as possible.
- The belayer must be able to see the belayed person.
- The belayer should be seated whenever possible.

3.1.10. A Useful Knot

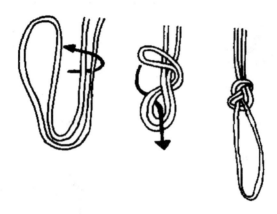

Figure of Eight on a bight. Creates a secure loop into which a person can step.

3.1.11. Belaying More Than One Person?

The loop must be quick to get in and out of and easy to adjust. Tie a figure of 8 on the rope and then a stopper knot above it.

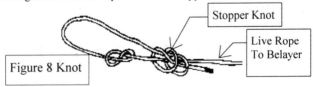

The party can then step in and out with ease and adjust the figure of 8 to achieve a perfect fit. The stopper knot sits comfortably against the figure of 8 knot thus forming a secure loop. It is worth ensuring everyone in the group can adjust the figure of 8 before the belay is set up above.

3.1.12. Lowering

This should be done only as a last resort and only for short steps. The easiest method of attaching the rope is by using a Thompson knot.

Take 5 lengths of the rope as shown, each length is equal to the height of the tallest person in the group.

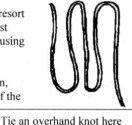

Tie an overhand knot here

Thus creating 2 short loops for the arms and 2 longer loops for the legs.

The knot should sit comfortably at sternum level.

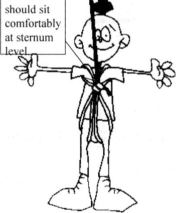

If there is more than one person to be lowered, this knot need only be made once then adjusted for each person. in turn. Adjust the loops by tying overhand knots in either the arm or leg loops as appropriate. The harness thus created should be tight but not unduly uncomfortable.

3.1.13. Caring For The Rope

It is normally best for the rope to be stowed away out of view. The rope should be regularly inspected and not left to fester in the bottom of your rucksack. Ideally, it should be stowed in its own little rope bag and stuffed in as opposed to coiled in, this makes it easier to extract short lengths rapidly, typically for dog lead type of security.

3.2. Moving On Snow

3.2.0. Introduction

The aim of this section is to describe how to move safely on very
short but steep sections of snow. This is restricted to areas where
a slip would not result in a long slide on to dangerous terrain
below. It is assumed that you have an ice axe. Movement on long
sections of steep snow and ice using ice axe and crampons is
outside the scope of this book.

The ice axe is essential when you go out into the mountains as it
can be used to cut steps in short steep sections and it can be used
as an aid to balance. There are two aspects to moving on snow,
making your own foot steps and kicking or cutting steps for
others. helping others.

Kicking steps in snow is a quick and effective method for
traversing snow slopes. With practice a good kicking rhythm,
balance and posture will develop. Generally one kick should be
enough to form a step but occasionally a second or third may be
required. If more are required revert to cutting steps with your
ice axe.

When kicking steps be aware of the other walkers around you. If
you are at the front breaking the trail restrict your stride to that of
the smallest person in your group. Everyone following on behind
should use the steps already made as this is much less tiring.

3.2.1. Holding Your Ice Axe

Your axe has sharp points and edges so is
potentially dangerous. If the axe is not in use
stow it away on your ruck sack.

When carrying your axe for balance hold the
axe as shown with the spike facing backwards
to prevent snagging, and so that you can break
yourself in the event of a fall.

If you need it frequently but not all the time stow it between your shoulder blades and your rucksack as shown. This allows you to stow and retrieve your ice axe quickly without having to stop.

3.2.2. Step Kicking Up/Down The Slope

These methods are best if you need to gain or loose altitude quickly. When climbing face the slope square on and kick straight into the slope using your ice axe for balance.

Be aware of the angle that your boot enters the snow so that the best steps are made

Bad   Acceptable   Preferred

When descending the slope, you can either face in to the slope and use the same kicking action as above. Alternatively, you can face out from the slope and use a straight leg swinging action to dig your heels into the snow

3.2.3. Traversing Diagonally

Climbing diagonally is best used on longer sustained climbs although this can be very tiring on the edges of your feet. To avoid this switch back frequently. This allows you to use the outside and inside edge of each foot evenly and to rest when you change direction.

The pattern of steps will
look like this

On steep slopes the easiest method is to place
your ice axe high then kick two steps up to it.
The new step pattern is like this.

3.2.4. Step Cutting

When the snow becomes too
firm to kick or you need to
cross a small ice patch you may
have to cut steps with your axe.
When traversing diagonally
this may be a simple slash cut
where the cut is made in one
smooth action. The step is just
big enough to get the edge of
your boot in.

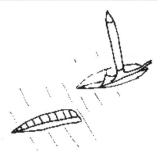

Alternatively you can dig a
foot sized firm step with two
or three cuts, these steps take
longer to construct and tiring
so they are probably best used
on very short sections of
steep, firm slope.

3.2.5. If You Fall On Snow

When you are moving on snow there is always a possibility of
falling. If you are not prepared, you could find yourself sliding
more and more rapidly towards dangerous ground and serious

injury. When you fall you must react quickly and positively to bring yourself to a stop. It is vital that you;

- Grasp your ice axe firmly in both hands.
- Roll over onto your stomach.
- With your head up hill.
- And your feet held clear of the snow.
- Bring your ice axe into your shoulder.
- Apply all your bodily weight over the ice axe.
- And press into the snow as hard as you are able to.
- To bring your self quickly to a stop.

In this head down position, thrust your ice axe out to the side and dig it deep into the snow. This action forces your feet to slide past so that your head is now up hill.

If you are on your back you must try and thrust your ice axe in to the snow to one side. Lean towards the axe to force it in to the snow. Your legs will slide into the down hill position. As they pass the ice axe role over onto your stomach. Continue to press your ice axe into the snow

Next, keeping your boots clear of the snow you must bring your ice axe into your shoulder, look away from your axe and curl up to put all your weight over the ice axe digging it deep into the snow.

It is vitally important that you continue to press hard into the snow until you come to a complete stop. Even when it seems that you are not stopping continue to press hard, it is generally better to collide with rocks or trees feet first.

Once you have come to a complete stop thrust your boots into the

snow to stop your self going any further. Uncurl slowly, releasing your weight off the ice axe a little at a time. Once you feel secure climb back up the slope to rejoin your party before continuing.

Being able to bring yourself to a complete stop is the most important skill that you must have if you travel on snow. It is worth practicing the techniques as frequently as you can so that your actions become automatic.

If you believe that a serious injury is likely if you are unable to stop your fall, then you should provide extra security using a rope.

3.3. Steep Ground Winter

3.3.0. Introduction

This section deals only with setting up quick, safe belays on snow and does not cover the realms of snow and ice climbing , mixed winter climbing or the use of crampons and ice axes. The factors for roping up in winter conditions are the same as for summer conditions. Deep and probably steep snow and short patches of ice may be encountered anywhere in the UK during winter.

3.3.1. Priorities For Belaying

Rock then Ice then Snow

3.3.2. Belays to Rock

Same principles as section 3.1. It is expected that people doing winter routes using a rope and requiring protection should have some experience of basic climbing techniques, i.e. placing runners and rope management.

In addition to rock spikes and threads the leader must know how to use a range of equipment and techniques used in climbing. It is assumed that this equipment plus karibiners and slings are to be carried. There is not enough space to cover the subject here, but there are some very good books in the references.

3.3.3. Anchoring on Ice

It is possible to construct your own anchor in the form of an ice bollard or to use natural features such as very large icicles. Climbing on steeper ice using ice screws, pitons and other devices is outside the scope of this book.

3.3.4. Types of Ice

A quick inspection of the ice gives an indication of how it was formed and how good it is likely to be. There are basically 6 types.

Eggshell Ice. Develops during freeze thaw conditions, and is essentially a thin ice layer over an air bubble. The ice may act like a small green house with the trapped air warming up and melting the under lying snow or ice. Generally unsafe.

Water Ice. Forms from flowing water and is transparent with no obvious crystal structure. Is hard and brittle, sometimes thin and hollow. The surface may shatter when struck with axe or crampons (dinner plating). Hard to get ice screws to seat or for building ice bollards.

Ice Crust. A thin film or crust of ice over snow formed by freeze thaw on the surface layer, normally associated with water from above adding thickness to the film of ice. Very brittle and deceptive. Avoid.

Verglas. Normally only up to 25 mm thick formed by melt and freeze over rock surfaces. Sticks like glue to all surfaces. Comes from either water from rain or from melting surface ice or from melt water from above. Is very tough. Hazardous to all.

White Ice. Formed from neve, hardened by water seeping into snow during frequent melt freeze conditions. Very stable and easy to work on. Ideal for walkers and climbers.

Blue Ice. Blue or possibly green colouration caused by increased density and greater water ice content in neve. Forms from water ice with snow plastered onto it. This increases the volume and gives it a good plastic feel. Safe and reliable.

3.3.5. Ice Bollard

Ice bollards are very reliable, they are small and easy to build. Use natural features when ever possible. A guide line for size is based on the condition of the ice.

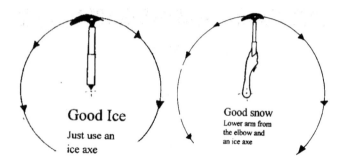

Good Ice

Just use an
ice axe

Good snow
Lower arm from
the elbow and
an ice axe

The bollard can be carved to a depth of as little as 5 cm depending on the condition of the ice. A lip is carved all the round as shown to prevent the rope from slipping out. Use the ice bollard for direct and indirect belays or abseil anchor. The shape is shown in profile.

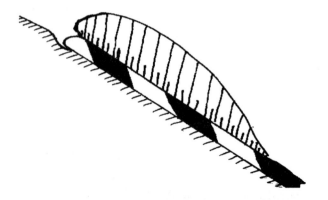

3.3.6. Belaying On Snow

Belaying on snow is more difficult than on ice because it is much less dense. One may set up a quick and easy belay using the following;

- Snow bollards.
- A bucket seat for a braced belay.
- The ice axe in combination with the boot.

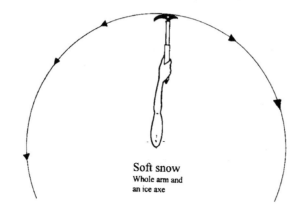

Soft snow
Whole arm and
an ice axe

The diagram above illustrates the size of bollard required. The bollard may be reinforced with ice axes rucksacks or other materials as shown below. Note that the bollard should only be as deep as the best layer that can be found in the snowpack. This effectively means from a few cms to perhaps 0.5m or more.

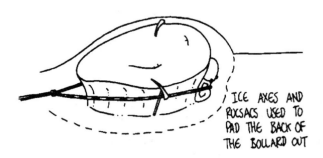

ICE AXES AND RUCSACS USED TO PAD THE BACK OF THE BOLLARD OUT

3.3.8. The Bucket Seat Belay

This belay takes a few minutes to set up because of the need to dig a bucket shaped hole. It is a practical method when the snow is deep but not firm enough for the foot and axe brake or the stomper belays listed below.

The belayer digs a bucket shaped hole in the snow then adopts a seated braced belay position. The seat is very secure due to the depth and shape of the bucket seat as shown.

3.3.9. Foot & Axe Break

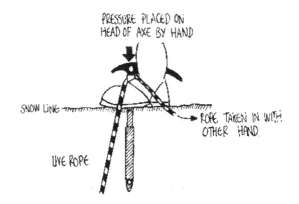

PRESSURE PLACED ON
HEAD OF AXE BY HAND

SNOW LINE

ROPE TAKEN IN WITH
OTHER HAND.

LIVE ROPE

This is a very quick and efficient way of belaying someone up a very short difficult step. Time is of the essence here as it only takes a few seconds to embed the shaft in the firm snow pack and pass the rope around it. The foot braced against the axe reduces the risk of the axe being pulled out of the snow.

3.3.10. The Stomper

A refinement of the foot and axe method is the stomper belay. This is used for longer difficult steps on good firm snow. It is used either to help someone up or to lower them. The stomper is very quick to set up and has the advantage that the belayer is standing and has easier observation.

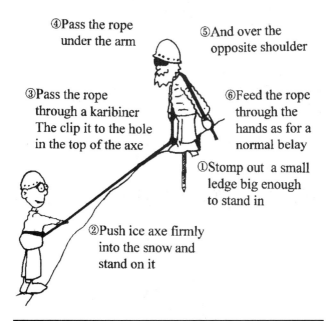

④Pass the rope under the arm

⑤And over the opposite shoulder

③Pass the rope through a karibiner The clip it to the hole in the top of the axe

⑥Feed the rope through the hands as for a normal belay

①Stomp out a small ledge big enough to stand in

②Push ice axe firmly into the snow and stand on it

3.3.11. Embedded Ice Axe Belays

These are more complex methods of belaying on snow when greater security is required. They are used more as a technique for climbing steeper, longer and more difficult snow pitches. They are outside the scope of this book and are not considered further.

3.4. River Crossing

River crossings are those where the party has to stop and consider the options and where mistakes could result in an emergency situation, i.e. the river is too wide to leap across and the water is greater than knee deep.

> # Avoid river crossings if you can

3.4.1. Planning Ahead

Forewarned is forearmed. Be aware of the weather forecast and keep an eye on the weather at all times. Identify possible danger areas from the map and try to avoid the possibility of having to make a crossing. If there is a big river to cross, and the weather forecast is poor, consideration should be given to amending your plans.

If you are confronted with a swollen river, avoid making an unsafe crossing. Check the map upstream and downstream for a bridge or other likely crossing places. Alternatively, consider waiting for the water level to drop. A river crossing should only be considered if the alternatives present greater hazard.

3.4.2. Selecting A Crossing Point

The best place to cross is at the riffles as shown on the diagram below. Water accelerates into bends causing deep pools against the outside bank. The water then slows as it enters the relatively much shallower riffle.

- The river bed and the bank should be as level as possible and free from obstructions.
- If there are islands use these to cross, but take care.
- The entry and exit point should be low enough for easy use.
- Are there suitable anchor points close by for belays?

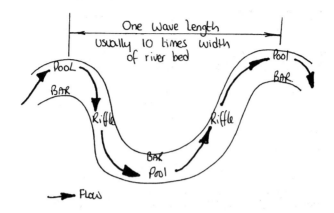

One wave length
usually 10 times width
of river bed

Pool

BAR

Riffle

Pool

BAR

Riffle

BAR

Pool

→ Flow

3.4.3. Prepare For The Crossing

After selecting the crossing point consideration should be given to briefing the group and preparing their gear.

In particular, brief them on what to do if they have problems in the water and get swept away.

If the crossing is quite deep and wide, consider changing into a full set of waterproofs and trainers to make the crossing. All dry, warm clothing should be stowed away in the rucksack. If you decide to do this change quickly on the other bank.

3.4.4. Making The Crossing

- Always face into the current with bent knees and move steadily checking the river bed before each step and avoid crossing your legs.
- Rucksack straps should be loosened off and waist straps undone. If you fall in shed your rucksack immediately. Don't panic and don't fight against the current. As you are swept away, try to get your feet pointing downstream and keep an eye out for obstacles and try to avoid getting caught up in overhanging or submerged branches.
- To escape the current make bold thrusts for the exit bank or, if you are on a rope, allow yourself to be pulled in.

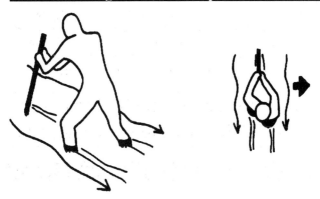

Individual Side Shuffle. Facing into the current, use a large stick for balance. Small groups of 4 - 5 people can make a crossing together using any number of variations of the huddle method illustrated below. The principles are the same for which ever method you use.

3.4.6. The Huddle Method

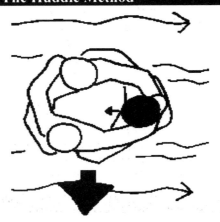

The Huddle. For up to 4 or 5 people. All facing each other and bracing against the current to form a stable body. Controlled by the person facing upstream (shaded head).

3.4.7. Crossing Using Ropes

Crossing a river is potentially dangerous at any time. The use of a rope aids the crossing but may present a new set of dangers. The rope should be a minimum of 3 times longer than the width of the crossing. The essential methods are based on continuous loops or on tensioned rope methods. Two examples are illustrated below.

> # You must have a method to cut the rope quickly should the need arise.

3.4.8. Continuous Loop

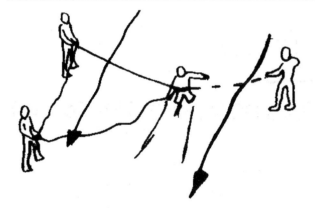

This is the simplest and quickest method using one rope. The upstream belayer controls the crossing whilst the down stream belayer takes the tension only if the person making the crossing is washed away. If there are enough people and the rope is long enough establish an upstream belayer on both banks.

3.4.9. Tensioned Rope Method

The use of 2 ropes improves flexibility and allows the party to cross wider rivers. The person making the crossing has the tensioned rope for support whilst the other rope is used to haul them to the bank if there are difficulties.

3.4.10. After The Crossing

- Change rapidly into dry warm clothing.
- Consider moving away quickly to get everyone warm again and then finding a more sheltered location for hot drinks and food.
- If anyone fell in the water treat them as quickly as possible and remain alert to the possibility of hypothermia.

4. Winter

4.0. Introduction

There is nothing more rewarding than a sunny, crisp winter day in the snow covered mountains. But the shorter days, and generally cold and windy weather, demand a higher level of skill and fitness than is required in summer. There must also be an ever vigilant awareness of avalanche.

4.1. This section looks at the factors associated with snow and what you can do to evaluate the conditions. It may help you decide whether to set out or not, and what to watch for when on the move.

The aim is to make your next winter trip to any wild area as rewarding and enjoyable as possible. It is better to err on the side of caution no matter how far you have just travelled to get there. The mountains will still be there tomorrow.

4.2. Travelling in the mountains in winter demands awareness of the risks. Apart from the hazards associated with mountain weather and terrain there is the specially relevant hazard of avalanche. This section describes avalanches, avalanche terrain, slopes where they may start and avalanche warning signs.

4.3. Knowing where to look and how to search after an avalanche, coupled with quick determined reactions can save lives. Time is against you, victims must be found and rescued if they are to have any chance. The essential survival strategy is to avoid being caught or buried.

4.1. Snow Condition.

4.1.0. Snow Condition

Having decided to venture out there are several things which you can do to assess and continually reassess the condition of the snow pack. These include observing the weather, keeping an eye on the terrain and testing the snow pack yourself.

4.1.1. Snowpack Condition - Indicators

- The presence of fresh or still falling unconsolidated snow is a cause of some concern as most avalanches occur during or just after snowstorms. Slopes take 2-3 days to settle (longer if in shadow).
- Snow fall of 2 cm per hour or greater increases avalanche hazard. 30 cms+ of new snow may give rise to powder avalanches.
- Prolonged low temperatures prolong avalanche hazard.
- Sudden increase in temperature including warm winds, thawing or rain onto unconsolidated snow increases the risk of sudden avalanche.
- Recent avalanches indicate unstable snow conditions for areas at the same altitude and exposure elsewhere.
- Large, natural snowballs rolling down slopes, sudden collapse of crust under your feet, hollow sounds, cracks appearing in the snow, signs of melt, mini slabs forming under the weight of skis or boots all indicate that the snow pack is changing and becoming unstable.

4.1.2. The Shovel and Hand Shear Test

The best avalanche prediction information comes from local sources combined with local weather records and avalanche data. There are no rules of thumb. If you cannot acquire local information test the snow pack yourself.

This test is restricted to locating and testing hard layers in the snow. It is quick and easy to do but can be impractical on deep soft snow. All parties travelling in winter conditions should have at least one snow shovel.

The test can be done using the hands too. It should be repeated nearby to confirm the result. With practice the test takes less than 5 minutes. Great care should be exercised when interpreting results. A complete picture includes weather history and knowledge of the terrain.

Dig a pit then cut a block as shown below. Place the shovel or your hands down the back of the block and gently apply pressure, increase the pressure and note the point at which the block fails.

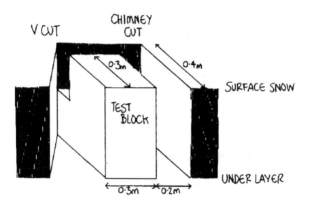

4.1.3. Risk Assessment

Degree Of Risk

Very High	Test block fails during cutting or insertion of shovel
High	Test block fails with slight shovel pressure
Moderate	Test block fails under moderate shovel pressure
Low	Test block fails under firm but sustained pressure
Minimal	Failure of the test block is difficult to induce

4.1.4. Rutschblock - Walking Shear Test

This is a variant of the Ski Shear Test (Rutschblock) and is being developed by Avalex (Caledon, West Terrace, Kingussie, Inverness-Shire PH21 1HA). It is included here as another option for mountain users.

Firstly dig a pit 1.5 meters wide then cut a 1meter square block as shown in the uphill side of the pit.

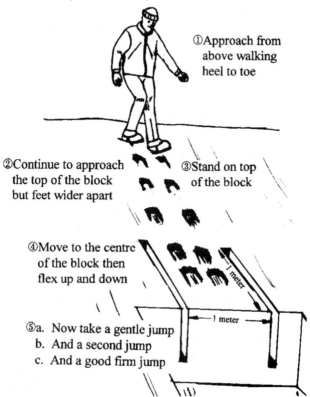

①Approach from above walking heel to toe

②Continue to approach the top of the block but feet wider apart

③Stand on top of the block

④Move to the centre of the block then flex up and down

⑤a. Now take a gentle jump
b. And a second jump
c. And a good firm jump

1 meter

1 meter

4.1.5. Failure Description & Risk Assessment

Degree Of Risk

Very High	Block fails during digging, cutting or at step 1
High	Block fails at step 2
Moderate	Block fails at step 3
Low	Block fails at step 4
Minimal	Block fails at any of the moves at step 5

Snow & Avalanche Reports are available daily from mid December to mid April from the Police/SAIS Information line Telephone - Free, **0800 0960 007**, Local Radio and National Newspapers.

Also available via email **avalanche@dcs.gla.ac.uk** .

The latest forecast is posted in pubs, climbing shops, and in the car parks near to the areas the forecasts are for.

Areas covered by the Scottish Avalanche Information Service (SAIS)

Glen Coe - Observations from Glen Coe and Glen Etive.
Lochaber - Observations from Ben Nevis and Aonach Mor.
Northern Cairngorm - Observations from the Northern Corries and Loch Avon.
Southern Cairngorm - Observations on Lochnagar, in Glenshee, and some coverage of the Southern Cairngorms
Creag Meagaidh - Observations on Creag Meagaidh and some surrounding hills.

You can also report avalanche activity via SAIS web site or by printing out the form and sending it by post or fax.

To get the most from the Snow & Avalanche Report look at;

- Date and time of issue (information for each report is gathered as late as conditions allow during the day).
- Avalanche hazard for the day of issue. This reflects conditions on a scale of 1(low risk) to 5 (very high risk). The report has a general report on the highest hazard areas and detail of observed avalanche. The hazard factor given refers to the highest hazard areas.
- Avalanche outlook for the next day following this report. It includes a hazard factor outlook. This hazard outlook only remains accurate if the weather forecast is correct. If the weather changes, or is not accurate make your own judgment to assess how the avalanche warnings will be affected.

The European Avalanche Hazard Scale

Hazard	Snowpack Stability	Avalanche Trigger
LOW (Category 1)	Generally well bonded and stable	Possible only with high additional loads on a few very steep extreme slopes. A few small natural sluffs possible
MODERATE (Category 2)	Moderately bonded on some steep slopes, otherwise generally well bonded	Possible with high additional loads particularly on the steep slopes indicated on the report. Large natural avalanches not likely
CONSIDERABLE (Category 3)	Moderately to weakly bonded in most places	Sometimes low additional loads. Report may indicate many slopes which are particularly affected. In some conditions, large to medium natural avalanches may occur
HIGH (Category 4)	Weakly bonded in most places	Probable with low additional loads on many steep slopes. In some conditions frequent medium & large natural avalanches may occur
VERY HIGH (Category 5)	Generally weakly bonded & largely unstable	Numerous natural large avalanches are likely even on moderately steep terrain

Notes

1. Additional loads.
   - **High** - Groups of walkers, climbers or skiers.
   - **Low** - A walker, climber or skier.

2. Cornice collapse is a specialised type of avalanche often independent of general avalanche hazard. When cornice danger is known to exist, it will be specified in the report. Avoid cornices altogether if you can.

4.1.7. Preparing For Winter Travel

- Be aware of the avalanche hazard (see 6.1.5. above).
- Gather as much local information as you can.
- Analyse recent weather patterns and available snow data.
- Analyse the route and terrain you intend to use and aim to minimize risk and hazards.
- Have a safety and rescue plan and know what to do in an emergency.
- Carry and know how to use your safety equipment.
- Keep equipment in good working order.
- Be alert at all times and expect the worst.

4.1.8. Travelling Precautions

- Whilst on the move it is essential to be observant of the weather and the snow conditions.
- Do not travel alone.
- Maintain a reasonable distance between each other, exposing only 1 person at a time on potential avalanche paths.
- Watch for avalanche whilst crossing risky areas and keep a watch on individuals crossing these places.
- Do not stop in hazard areas. For the crossing undo rucksack waist belt and loosen straps and wear jackets, mitts and hats done up.
- If you decide to belay someone across a gap, the belay must be on rock or tree and must be bomb proof.
- The belayer is to use an independent belay rope.
- Select routes carefully avoiding likely trigger points.
- Rests and campsites must be in known safe areas.

4.1.9. Danger Zones

Choosing absolutely safe routes in avalanche terrain is frequently very difficult. In most cases you must cross or climb up or down steep ground to gain ridge routes. General areas to be aware of are;

- Areas of deposited snow, cornices, gullies, cwms and corries
- Slopes facing the sun
- Short very steep hills such as old mine workings and glacial moraines
- Convex slopes and the bottom of steep slopes

- Narrow valleys, and deep depressions
- Lee slopes are frequently overloaded and subsequently unsafe
- Open forest on steep slopes
- North facing slopes may remain unstable for long periods
- Be very careful where other walkers have passed, as they may have weakened the snowpack
- Slopes between 30° & 45°

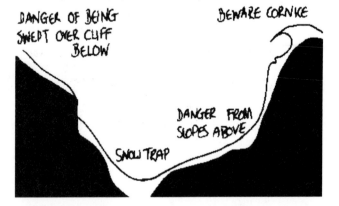

4.1.10. Potential Safe Ground

No terrain is to be considered totally safe. Some can be described as potentially safer. These are;

- High points and ridges (beware cornices)
- Wide valleys and areas beyond visible runout zones and avalanche cones
- Gentle slopes with no steep slopes above
- Dense forest
- Concave slopes (but beware of steep slopes above)

Route selection is very difficult in winter because of ever changing conditions and potentially impractical detours. The aim therefore is to choose a practical route and be aware at all times of the dangers. Micro navigation becomes very important. Risk can be minimised and potentially dangerous slopes crossed keeping exposure to a minimum.

Do I need to cross?
Where should I cross?

Potentially dangerous terrain should be crossed before sunrise while the snowpack is relatively stable. During the day the condition of slopes will change as the sun passes over.

The diagram below shows the main features of the crossing. The slope remains unstable for quite some time during the daytime, until the temperature drops and the snow pack stabilises.

A sensible plan is to identify potentially dangerous slopes from the map and by asking locally. This saves time because suitable detours can be planned in advance.

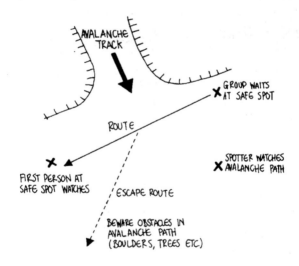

4.2. Avalanche

4.2.0. Types Of Avalanche

	Dry Powder Avalanche
Description	Northern slopes. Small powder movements from a single source. Spreads out as it gathers speed
Indications	Prolonged cold period below -4°C and snowfall in excess of 2 cm per hour.
Trigger	New snow accumulation, as little as 20 cm in start zone.
Effect	Tends to be surface movement only. Speed over 45m per second (100mph). Greatest cause of death is asphyxiation.
Assessment	Normally occur during or just after snow fall.

	Soft Slab Avalanche
Description	Most common avalanche. All slopes.
Indications	Heavy snowfall accompanied by winds 16-48 Kph. Force 3-6.
Trigger	Normally the victim. May trigger other weaknesses in the snowcap.
Effect	As little as 20 cm deep slab surface moves but may develop into a mixed slab & powder fall.
Assessment	Beware of drifts, lee slopes and under cornices, even if there is no recent snow.

	Hard Slab Avalanche
Description	Often hidden by fresh snow. May be several hard and soft layers.
Indications	Rapid changes in temperature.
Trigger	Often the victim.
Effect	Loud cracking noise. Hard layers crack to give large, sharp angular blocks. Frequently accompanied by large clouds of softer snow from sub layers.
Assessment	Shovel shear test or Rutschblock test.

Climax Avalanche

Description	Whole slope gives way. Often very large scale. Variety of conditions within the snowpack.
Indications	Very difficult to recognise. Prolonged cold spells more than 10 days below -4° C.
Trigger	As little as a 2°C rise in tempertaure. Modest fresh snow or drift on lee slopes.
Effect	Very large and destructive.
Assessment	Local knowledge of terrain and weather is essential. May occur during or just after snow fall.

Wet or Slush Avalanches

Description	Starts very slowly at first so easy to escape but gathers speed rapidly.
Indications	Common in spring or during prolonged warm spells accompanied by warm winds.
Trigger	Water weakens the snow pack structure during rapid rise in temperature.
Effect	On slopes as low as 20°. Very destructive. Sets like concrete when it stops.
Assessment	May be some small scale snowballing rolling down slopes. Also small scale local avalanches.

Ice Avalanche

Description	Very obvious overhanging ice such as frozen waterfalls collapsing.
Indications	Falls may occur night and day. Beware of thaw or rain.
Trigger	Very difficult to predict. Climbers have been known to trigger collapses.
Effect	Large blocks of ice dislodging earth and rock to tumble great distances. Frequently triggering other avalanches.
Assessment	Expect ice falls 24 hours a day every day. Beware of ice with water flowing on or in it.

4.2.1. Describing An Avalanche

Avalanches may be described in any combination as;

- **Type**   Loose Snow   or   Slab
- **Depth**   Full Depth   or   Surface
- **Snow**   Dry   or   Wet
- **Track**   Channelled   or   Unconfined
- **Moves by**   Flowing   or   Airborne

Note that avalanches by their nature are complex phenomena and are difficult to categorise specifically.

4.2.2. Start Zone - Slope Angles

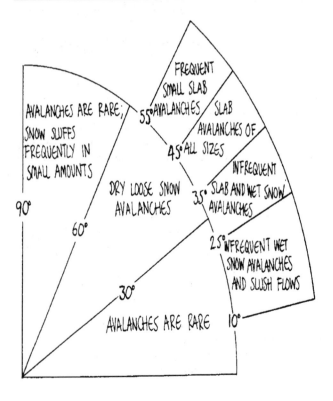

4.3. Avalanche Survival

4.3.0. How Deep Is The Victim Buried?

The victim's survival depends on how deep they are buried and how long they remain buried for.

Depth Of Burial	Chance of Survival
Remain on surface	Good (80% or better)
Partially buried	Poor (40 to 45%)
Totally buried	Very Poor (Less than 20%)

4.3.1. Cause Of Death

Cause of Death	%
Suffocation	65%
Collision with obstacles	25%
Hypothermia & shock	10%

4.3.2. Victim Survival Chance With Time

Buried Up to	Surface	Less Than 1 meter	1 to 3 meters	Over 3 meters
0 mins	up to 90%	80% +	60% +	less than 60%
30 mins	up to 75%	60% +	40% +	less than 40%
1 hour	up to 65%	50% +	20% +	less than 20%
1½ hours	up to 55%	35% +	5% +	less than 5%
2 hours	up to 40%	20% +	almost none	almost none

- The chance of survival diminishes rapidly with time.
- The deeper the victim the poorer the odds.
- It is vital that every party has a self rescue plan.
- After an avalanche the priority is to locate and rescue the victim.

4.3.3. If You Get Caught in an Avalanche

- **As the avalanche starts** Try to escape to the sides or behind natural shelter, i.e. boulders and trees.
- **Call out to attract attention before being engulfed** Then close your mouth and cover your nose. Try to remain upright by using a swimming motion.
- **As you feel the avalanche slowing down** Make a strong thrust for the surface and try to make an air space in front of your face.
- **When the motion stops, which way up am I?** To find out, dribble some spit, if it goes down your chin then you are upright. If it goes up your face, then you are upside down. If you can move, try to dig yourself out (in the opposite direction to the way the spit went). If not, listen for approaching rescuers and shout out when they are very near. Save oxygen by remaining calm, do not fight the sensation of blacking out.
- If there is a search and rescue dog, let it lick your face as its reward for finding you.

If You Are The Survivor

4.3.4. Survivor - Immediate Action Plan

- Stay calm, act methodically, ensure rest of party are safe and move to a safe place if necessary. Determine who is lost.
- Immediately note the last seen location of the victim(s) and try to determine where the victim may have come to rest.
- Assess further hazard and post a spotter to warn of further avalanches.
- Ensure everyone is aware of the search plan and the escape routes in the event of a second avalanche.
- Make a visual search of the avalanche debris, looking for signs of the victim such as limbs and equipment. Leave the evidence in place for reference and then listen.

4.3.5. Likely Burial Areas

Generally it will be quite difficult to determine where the victim is. Be methodical, stay calm and search the most likely areas first.

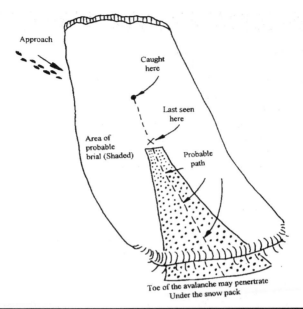

Approach

Caught
here

Last seen
here

Area of
probable
brial (Shaded)

Probable
path

Toe of the avalanche may penertrate
Under the snow pack

4.3.6. Searching For Victims - One Searcher

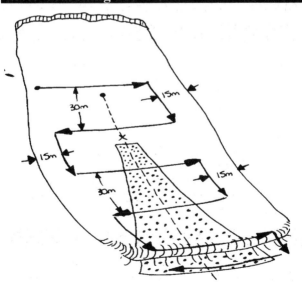

30m

15m

15m

30m

15m

81

4.3.7. Two Searchers

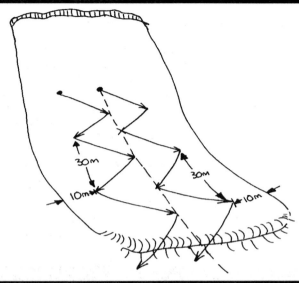

4.3.8. More Than Two Searchers

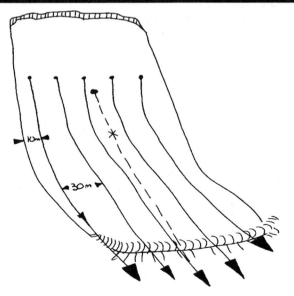

4.3.9. If After 1 Hour...

If after 1 hour you cannot find the victim;

- **Stop.** Ensure the remainder of the party are physically okay.
- Fill in the accident report form and send for assistance.
- Reassess the situation and resume the search.
- If Search and Rescue Dogs (SARDA) are expected, continue the search for as long as possible. It takes about 15mins after you have moved off the area before they can begin their work. The handler will brief you and direct you down wind of the search area.
- During all phases of the search keep the area as free from personal debris as possible, including food and patches of urine. These will hamper the dogs.
- Keep an eye on everyone. The combined effect of cold, shock and exhaustion induced by the incident cannot be over estimated. You must not allow others to become casualties too.

4.3.10. Care Of The Victim

- **ABC**
- **Check for and treat bleeding and breakages**
- **Treat for hypothermia and shock**

If the victim was found in the first hour and you did not send for help you must now consider the following courses of action;

- Do you need assistance with evacuation?
- Do you attempt self evacuation?

4.3.11. Essential Equipment

When travelling in winter, in addition to all the extra equipment that you are carrying you must consider a snow shovel as an essential item. A collapsible probe may is also worth considering.

5. Actions If !

5.0. Introduction

Getting lost followed by benightment are the most likely
emergency situations to develop. With a few basics skills you
should be able to reduce the trauma of such a situation. Knowing
what to do when it is dark and wet and when everyone is
exhausted, can lessen the impact of a potentially serious situation.

Equally, accidents can happen at any time and to anyone, alerting
the emergency services with the right information can save time
and possibly lives.

There are 4 basic principles to surviving these situations;

- Keep calm
- Stay together
- Think
- Try to help yourself

5.1. You Are Lost

When you finally admit that you
are lost....

1. Stop. Don't panic. Don't
rush. **Keep everyone together**.

2. Get your map out and try to
work out where you are.
Decide where on the map you
last knew your exact position.

3. Try to recount the type of terrain you travelled across. Take
into account how long you have been travelling for. Try to work
out roughly where you are. Use as much information as is
available to you. DO NOT get a fixation on one particular feature
and do not try to make the ground around you fit what is on the
map.

4. Decide what you are going to do. Some possibilities are;

- Return to your last known point and start again.
- Look for a safe way down.
- Aim for an obvious easily identifiable feature and try to re-establish your position.
- Or use your compass and pacing to determine how far and in what direction you are travelling.
- Do not rely on your sense of direction.

5. When you reach safety phone your contact and let them know that you are off the mountain and where you are. The likelihood is that you are miles from your intended destination.

6. If all this fails or the weather is so bad that you decide to stay put you are now in an enforced night out situation. You must move quickly to find or build an emergency shelter.

7. If you are well equipped the Mountain Rescue Team may wait for first light before starting a search. If you are not so well equipped they may decide to start a search immediately. If you have not left details of your route with someone then you may now be in a very serious and threatening situation.

5.2. You Need An Emergency Shelter

Okay, you are now caught out in the dark. Don't be too down hearted. Assess the situation. What state of fitness and morale are the group in? Is an attempted escape safer then staying? Consider the whole group, can they all make it off the hill safely? When you decide to stay put work logically and with urgency.

- **Seek shelter from the wind**. Build a wall if necessary, in winter dig a snow shelter.
- **Spare clothing**, should be shared evenly amongst the group. Put it all on. Use the rucksack and liner too. Loosen tight clothing such as belts and laces.
- **Insulate the ground**. Sit on any available padding. Sleeping mats and ropes for example.
- **Survival Bag/Space Blanket**. USE THEM. That's what you bought them for. Get as many people in each one as possible. (Group Emergency Shelters are extremely useful.)

- **Food and Drink**. Share equally amongst the group. Eat in small amounts regularly through the night. Did you remember your emergency rations?

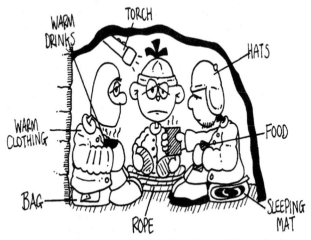

Emergency shelters can be long, cold, tedious affairs and other people are going to be worried. So,

- **Keep morale up** by singing, telling jokes or stories. Occasionally stretch arms and legs.
- Don't be selfish. **Look after each other**, every one is suffering and there is probably at least one suffering more than you!
- **Beware of the risk of hypothermia** and know how to recognise and treat it. See section 6.2.4.
- **Do not** leave the area until you have told your contact that you are safe. There may be a mountain rescue team out looking for you.

If you are unable to move at dawn or send anyone for help, initiate the emergency distress signal, which is 6 blasts on a whistle, followed by 1 minute silence. Repeated. Or use 6 repetitions of any other signalling devise such as your torch. Keep the signal going until the rescue team have indicated that they can see you.

If you are the rescuer, it is usually best not to respond to the distress signal until you can see the victims.

5.3. Emergency Rations

Emergency rations are carried to enable you to survive for an unspecified length of time in traumatic conditions. They should be fairly light, stowed in a waterproof container and sealed. They should be inspected on a monthly basis and changed accordingly.

Aim to be able to survive for 24 hours. It sounds like a long time but the quantity of emergency rations needed is quite small. The best plan is to take things which you personally like to eat. Generally there are two elements to consider, high energy food (carbohydrates and fats) and comfort food, i.e. if you enjoy boiled sweets then include some.

It is usually best to include food which is easily shared out. Kendal mint cake, chocolate bars and glucose sweets all have their place.

If you are going out in winter or you expect bad weather then take a larger lunch pack, double your sandwiches and add two extra chocolate bars. Heavy fruit cake is also very nutritious and a real morale booster. Don't forget the flask too.

5.4. You Have An Accident Or Emergency

In the event of an accident or emergency all reasonable efforts should be made to resolve the situation yourself before resorting to calling out the emergency services. Consider the following:

- The nature of the casualties injuries.
- The fitness and morale of the party.
- Time, terrain and weather.
- Is assistance from others available?

Large parties (More than 4 people)

- Seek shelter.
- Warm clothing and sleeping bags to be given to the casualty and those staying behind.
- Accident Report Form (appendix A).
- Messengers go to nearest telephone (minimum 2 with the accident report

form). They should choose a safe route down and not rush.
- At the phone dial 999 and ask for the Police. Give the information on the accident report form. Stay by the phone.
- Consider getting as many of your party off the mountain with the messengers as is safe. A minimum of two stay with the casualty.

Small Parties (2-3 people)

Small parties should be more cautious and be prepared for the worst. You are more likely to survive if you have discussed the dangers before hand and know how to deal with them. Otherwise the smallest incident could become problematical. Consider;

- What are the difficulties of moving the casualty, the nature of their injuries and the possibility that they may lapse into unconsciousness?
- What is the likelihood of rescue if you stay put?
- What are your survival chances if you do not go for help?
- What are the risks and dangers for the person going for help?

Dilemma. Do you leave the casualty alone while going for help? If yes, give the casualty all the spare kit and food and tell them exactly what you are going to do. If you have a rope trail it out across the likely approach route so that rescuers might find it and be led to the casualty.

5.5. You Need To Build Snow Shelters

There are two instances when you may be building a snow shelter;

1. A planned snow shelter. You have all the equipment and the time to build one comfortable enough for several people. These shelters are frequently used as alternatives to tents and provide excellent protection.

2. An emergency shelter. To survive the cold you need;

- The will to survive
- Practice
- Experience

If there is a casualty or you are lost the risk of death may be high if you fail to act quickly. These can be group shelters or just big enough for one.

5.6. Snow Shelters - Some Basic Rules

The principles of building and occupying any type of snow shelter in any situation are essentially the same. These are;

- It is time consuming. Work as quickly as possible but do not exhaust yourself. Loosen off clothing whilst working. Avoid sweating too much.
- The best snow shelters are built into a snow drift. If this is not possible build walls out of blocks of snow or large snow balls. Use trees, boulders, walls and any other feature to give added protection and strength.
- Don't build the shelter too large or too small.
- If the worst comes to the worst and you cannot do any of these things try piling as much snow as possible around yourself to gain protection from the wind.
- It is going to be very uncomfortable, you should endeavour to build the best shelter you can.
- Use a snow shovel. If you do not have one, use your hands to dig and wear gloves.

Let others know you are there

- Mark the entrance hole.
- Link other shelters with a rope anchored to each entrance.

Entering the shelter

- Brush all snow off yourself and your equipment.
- Bring all equipment inside.
- Close the hole leaving a small gap to allow air in.

Inside the shelter

- Keep a digging tool handy in case you need to dig yourself out.
- Insulate the sleeping area with all available padding.

- Use a torch in preference to candles. If using a candle use only one at a time. If the candle is left alight one person should remain awake at all times.
- When cooking, increase ventilation and have only one stove burning at a time. Avoid having water boil or simmer for long periods.
- Regularly smoothing the roof of the shelter prevents dripping and produces an insulating crust of ice.
- Regularly check and clear the entrance hole of drifting snow.
- Before settling down remove damp clothing and boots. Place both in waterproof bags inside your sleeping bag.
- Put your dry gear on.
- If you have to leave the shelter at night, either leave a light on or run a rope out to guide you back.
- Sleep with your head towards the door.

The most common cause of accident in snow shelters is carbon monoxide poisoning. You must ensure adequate ventilation is maintained at all times whilst in the shelter. Be obsessive about this.

5.7. A One Person Emergency Snow Hole

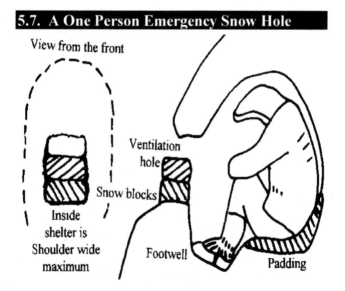

View from the front

Ventilation hole

Snow blocks

Inside shelter is Shoulder wide maximum

Footwell

Padding

6. First Aid

6.0. Introduction
6.1. The Essentials
6.2. Cold Injuries

6.0. Introduction

In towns and cities an ambulance is rarely more than 15 minutes away. Out in the mountains it could take several hours, especially if you have to go for help and the weather is very poor. It is essential, therefore, that you and the members of your party have a grasp of the fundamentals of First Aid. These are;

- Assess the situation
- Make the area safe for yourself and the casualty
- Assess all the casualties and give essential first aid
- Get help

You may have to look after the casualty and yourself for many hours in hostile conditions. Your job as a First Aider is to;

- **Preserve** life
- **Prevent** the situation deteriorating
- **Promote** recovery

Hopefully, you will never need to use your first aid skills. The fundamental things to bear in mind are that real first aid may be quite harrowing and situations may not be as clear cut as the spotlessly clean training rooms all over the nation.

But do take heart because most First Aiders respond extremely well to incidents, even when the scene is quite unpleasant. In addition, I have included a small section on emotional response to incidents and to the distressing situation of dealing with death.

> **Do not shy away from what you might see or hear, just do your best.**

6.1. The Essentials

Real first aid is not normally a nice thing to have to deal with. Knowledge and training coupled with practice will help you to face up to the reality of genuine suffering. First aid is about doing your best in the circumstances. There are risks, especially if medical help is many hours away.

Some casualties are not going to respond in a way that you expect, and the outcome might not be what you hoped for. It is possible that the casualty will die. If you believe that you have done your best and that what you did was correct then you must accept what has happened and have a clear conscience.

The one rule of thumb is - **Do No Harm**.

6.1.1. Priorities In First Aid (SLAP)

Safety **(In this order)**

- **Those in the group** (Do not create more casualties)
- **Yourself** (You must not become a casualty)
- **The casualty** (Are they safe from further danger?)

Life Saving First Aid **(In this order)**

- **CHECK**   Airways, Breathing, Circulation
- **DEAL WITH**   Serious Injuries
- **BE AWARE OF**   Shock

Action **P**lan. Weigh up the options and decide on a course of action (Self evacuation or stay put. Send or go for help.)

If sending for help use the most capable and fittest people in the party (minimum 2). Complete the Accident Report Form at appendix A and ensure it goes with the messengers.

If you are solo - treat yourself and make every effort to make good your own rescue. Do not depend on other people coming along and helping you.

6.1.2. A. B. C.

A is for Airway. Open the airway by tilting the head back and lifting the chin. If there is any debris in the mouth or throat tilt the casualty's head away from yourself and scoop the contents out with your fingers.

B is for Breathing. If the casualty is not breathing you must do it for them. With the head tilted back as in A, do mouth to mouth or mouth to nose resusitation.

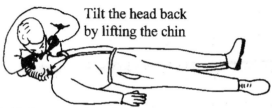

Tilt the head back
by lifting the chin

Pinch the nose closed
keep fingers away from the eyes

C is for Circulation. Keep blood circulating around the body by doing chest compression.

Lean over the casualty
lock your elbows and
press straight down

Place the heal of your
hand on the chest keeping
fingers clear

Release pressure by rocking back
Reapply pressure by rocking forward

6.1.3. Resuscitation

The aim of resuscitation is to get air into the lungs and to pump oxygenated blood round the casualty's body when they are unable to do it themselves. The actions are carried out consecutively, breaths first followed by chest compressions and are continued until the heart begins to beat without help and the casualty is able to breath unaided.

The first aider doing the breathing should control the situation. Resuscitation is very tiring so change places occaisionally. The number of breaths to chest compressions depends on the number of first aiders available.

- **1 First Aider** 2 breaths then 15 chest compressions.
- **2 First Aiders** 1 breath then 5 chest compressions.

- Breathing rate at 10 per minute (1 breath every 6 seconds)
- Chest compressions at 80 per minute (3 every 2 seconds)

6.1.4. Vital Signs

Vital signs are an indication of the body's general state. Checking and recording the vital signs is a crucial part of first aid and is of great importance to the medical services. They may be done at any time but must be recorded every 10 to 15 minutes.

Pulse
Adults 60-80/ min. Children 80-100/ min. Pulse rate increases with fear, anxiety and exercise, but it may be slower if the casualty is very fit. To find the pulse press two fingers on either side of the windpipe. This is the most reliable place to find the pulse.

Breathing
Adults 12-15/min, Children 20-30/min
Listen for irregularities such as gurgling or wheezing.

Skin
Warm and dry to touch with an underlying full colour (depending on ethnic origin of casualty). Caucasians go ashen or pale. Coloured skin may turn dull ashen grey, or a dull yellow brown. All skin types may also appear mottled and/or bluish. Make note of unduly hot or cool skin.

Eyes

Same size pupils both eyes, contracting evenly when exposed to direct light. Uneven or slow response in the pupils may indicate serious head injuries. To check response shade both eyes then expose to light or flash a torch in the eyes. They should react simultaneously, evenly and promptly.

Consciousness

Is the casualty fully alert and aware of time and place? Do they respond to verbal and physical stimuli? Is the casualty able to talk without slurred or difficult speech or confusion?

Pain & Movement

Does the casualty reacts to stimuli and move freely when instructed? A lack of reaction may indicate damage to the central nervous system. Even unconscious victims react to a painful stimulus. Ask the casualty to wiggle fingers and toes before trying legs and arms. See if they can grasp your hand or resist a push to the soles of the feet. If a fracture is suspected do not get the casualty to move that limb. Support any suspected neck or back injuries.

6.1.5. Observation Chart (Glasgow Version)

A copy of the chart is at appendix B1. During a prolonged incident it is vitally important the casualty is monitored continuously. This allows you to determine if their situation is improving or deteriorating and allows timely remedial action.

This chart was developed by medical professionals in accident and emergency units in Glasgow and is now widely used in first aid. The chart forms the basis of useful medical information and should accompany the casualty to hospital.

In the relevant box in each category enter;

- **Eyes, Movement & Speech.** Tick relevant box
- **Pulse. W** Weak, **S** Strong, **R** Regular, **B** Bounding
- **Breathing. Q** Quiet, **N** Noisy, **E** Easy, **D** Difficult

6.1.6. Observation Chart Notes

A copy is at appendix B2. These notes plus the completed chart above form an invaluable record for the medical services and are useful for making decisions about treatment and after care. Both pages form a single document with the observation chart on one side and these notes on the rear.

6.1.7. Signs & Symptoms. What Are They?

- **Signs.** These are things you can observe
- **Symptoms.** What the casualty feels or experiences

Look for signs, by applying the senses of sight, touch, hearing, smell.

Look and feel for; bleeding, swelling, tenderness, deformity, pale or flushed skin, sweating, rapid or slow breathing, raised or lowered body temperature, rapid or slow pulse, anxiety or pained expression, unusual movements anywhere on the body, grating bone ends, bleeding from any orifice, muscle spasm, response to touch, response to speech, foreign bodies, needle puncture marks, vomiting, incontinence, containers or other objects lying close by.

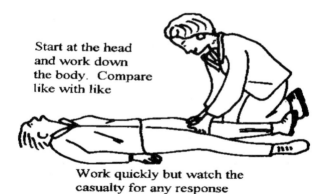

Start at the head and work down the body. Compare like with like

Work quickly but watch the casualty for any response

Smell for alcohol, acetone, burning, gas or fumes, solvents or glue and incontinence.

Listen for noisy or distressed breathing, groaning, sucking wounds, response to touch or speech.

Symptoms. Listen to what the casualty tells you. These include, pain, apprehension, heat, cold, loss of normal movement and sensation, abnormal movement or sensation, thirst, nausea, tingling, faintness, stiffness, weakness, dizziness, sensation of broken bones, memory loss and temporary unconsciousness.

Continuously check signs and symptoms at all stages of assessing the casualty.

6.1.8. Assessing The Casualty

It is of great importance to determine the extent of the injuries on each casualty. If there is more than one casualty this assessment will indicate the priority for treatment.

The basic principle is to establish contact with the casualty through speech and touch and to retain that link at all times. This link gives the casualty confidence in both you and the situation.

Aim to put pressure on yourself and <u>keep calm</u>. This check should take no longer than 2 minutes, work quickly but thoroughly. Don't rush. Be gentle but firm with your hands, speak to the casualty kindly but with purpose. The same action is carried out on both conscious and unconscious casualties.

Are you or the casualty in any further danger?

Assess Level Of Consciousness. Establish this by;

- Hello my name is....
- I am a First Aider.
- Tell the casualty what you are doing.
- Keep talking to the casualty at all times even if there is no apparent response.
- Keep pressure on yourself.

Continue to reassure the casualty by asking lots of questions. Questioning encourages a response from the casualty which helps you to determine their level of consciousness, never let them feel alone.

If casualty is unconscious check;

Airways   **Breathing**   **Circulation**.

Speak to the casualty. Look and touch where you are inspecting and listen. Ask the casualty the following; where does it hurt? Where does it hurt the most? Is it constant or intermittent pain? Are you on any medication? Do you have diabetes or asthma?

Remove false teeth and contact lenses if possible. Check the vital signs above and below any injury site as you come to them.

The examination is achieved by comparing opposite sides so the hands are run down both sides of the head and trunk or down each side of each limb simultaneously.

- **Head.** Skull, scalp, eyes, check that the pupils are the same size and that they respond to light. Get the casualty to follow your finger by moving their eyes only. They should move together in the same direction. Look in the ears and mouth but do not move the head during examination.
- **Neck.** Pulse and vital signs again. Do not move the spine.
- **Face.** Check for asymmetry and facial movements.
- **Collar bones and shoulders.**
- **Arms**. Check together for deformity, then individually.
- **Outside shoulder and under the armpits.**
- **Hands**. If there is no obvious fracture, have the casualty try to grip your hand then push against your hand.
- **Down side of chest**.
- **Chest and back** (Slide hands under back. Not Spine)
- **Abdomen.** Should be soft to the touch. Suspect serious injury if sensitive, or rigid, or casualty in pain. Blood in stools or urine, and open abdominal wounds are very serious.
- **Pelvis.** Press down gently on the pubic arch, if there is a response diagnose a fracture then move to the legs. If there is no response press gently on both sides and note any response.
- **Legs.** Compare left and right together, then one leg at a time, front and back, then knee, shin and calf.
- **Feet and ankles.** Compare left and right together. Do not attempt to remove boots. To test for a reaction tap the sole of the casualty's boot with your knuckle and note any response. Ask the casualty to push or pull against your hand with the foot, but only if there is no obvious fracture.
- **Now go back to the head and face. Speak to the casualty.**
- **Spinal inspection.** Do not move the casualty.

Stand up and stretch before continuing. Tell the casualty what you believe the problem is. Tell the casualty what your intentions are. Strengthen the bond between the casualty and yourself. Now treat the injuries in the order of priority determined by the inspection.

SPEAK TO CASUALTY CONTINUALLY

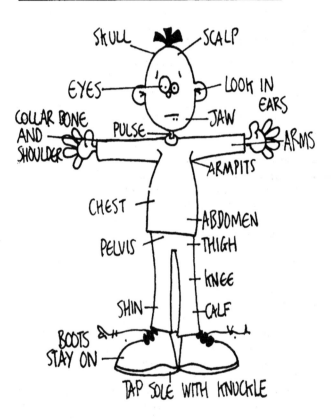

6.1.9. The Recovery Position

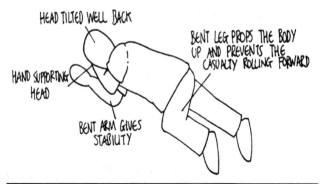

HEAD TILTED WELL BACK

BENT LEG PROPS THE BODY UP AND PREVENTS THE CASUALTY ROLLING FORWARD

HAND SUPPORTING HEAD

BENT ARM GIVES STABILITY

6.1.10. Shock

Shock accompanies most accidents. It is caused by reduced blood pressure after heart attack or more commonly by loss of bodily fluid by bleeding (internal and external). Shock is the body's automatic self defence mechanism to keep the vital organs alive. To do this it withdraws all fluids from the extremities and sends them to where they are needed most.

6.1.11. Shock - Signs & Symptoms

Early Signs

Rapid pulse
Sweating

Cold and clammy
Thirst
Pale gray skin (Check inside lip, finger nail or ear lobe)

Intermediate Signs

Fast irregular pulse
Nausea and vomiting

Weak and giddy
Rapid, shallow breathing

Advanced Signs

Restless and anxious
Yawning (Air Hunger)
Breathing and heart may stop

Aggressive
Unconsciousness

6.1.12. Treating Shock

- Reassure continuously. (Never leave the casualty unattended.)
- No food or drink. (You may wet the lips.)
- Treat the injuries. (ABC, breakages, burns and any others.)
- Lay the casualty down.
- Keep head low, raise and support legs.
- Loosen tight clothing. (Neck, chest, waist.)
- Insulate casualty from cold (including ground) and keep warm.
- Observe and record responsiveness. (Use observation chart.)
- Be prepared to resuscitate.

6.1.13. Sprains & Strains - (RICE)

For sprains and strains RICE is a useful 4 step guide to treatment.

- **R**est the injured limb to prevent further injury.

- **I**ce - if available, or snow wrapped in a towel and placed around the injury site for at least 30 minutes. A towel soaked in cold water may also help.

- **C**ompression - firm bandaging of the injury further restricts swelling. Check the pulse below the injury site frequently and adjust if necessary.

- **E**levate the affected limb. Reevaluate every 30 minutes.

The casualty may be able to walk with some assistance, if so make your way off the mountain. If the casualty can not walk then RICE again for a further 30 minutes. If there is no improvement treat the injury as a break and either attempt to evacuate or send for assistance.

6.1.14. Securing Broken Limbs

The general principles for dealing with fractures are as follows;

- **Support the affected limb**.

- **Do not move the limb unnecessarily**. The casualty may be unwilling to let you if they are conscious.
- **Do not move the casualty unnecessarily.**

- **Use plenty of padding** on bony parts of the effected limb, above and below the injury, and in all the hollows.
- **Immobilise the limb by securing:**
Legs to the good leg
Arms to the body
Use splints if available and appropriate
- **Secure firmly with broad bandages,** (as many as is comfortable for the casualty) above and below the injury site. With leg and pelvic injuries tie the ankles firmly to aid the splinting process.
- **If you use a sling to support arm fractures** place plenty of padding between arm and body then immobilise using a broad bandage over the sling, but under the good arm.
- **Work** from the casualty's injured side.
- **Tie knots** on the uninjured side.
- **Monitor the limb** on the side furthest from the heart (the fingers on an arm injury or the toes on a leg injury). Watch for loss of circulation and pulse. Ease bandages if they are restricting blood flow.
- **Shock** may develop quickly.
- **Arrange** to evacuate to hospital urgently.
- **Treat as a stretcher case** unless the casualty is willing to attempt to walk off and there are no further risks.

6.1.15. An Improvised Stretcher

Carrying a stretcher is hard work, carrying an improvised one is also painful for all concerned. Line the stretcher with sleeping mats, sleeping bags or any other padding. Keep a close watch over the casualty by checking them continuously. One person must take command. The simplest improvised stretcher is made using your emergency bivi bag some pebbles and rope or string.

Lay the bivi bag out flat. Place a pebble or similar object in each corner and down the sides as shown and secure each one with a piece of string, or if available your rope. Using your 9mm rope has the advantage of providing additional hand holds as illustrated. There are many other types of improvised stretchers, this method is the simplest.

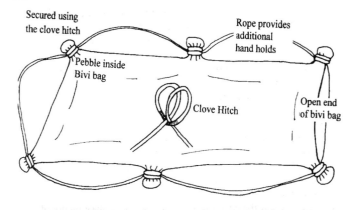

Secured using the clove hitch

Rope provides additional hand holds

Pebble inside Bivi bag

Clove Hitch

Open end of bivi bag

6.1.16. Emotional Response

First aid incidents are stressful and often very frightening. The victim's response to the incident is of great importance. A will to survive and positive attitude will help both the victim, the First Aider and the rescuers. It is essential to promote this positive attitude to gain the casualty's confidence. A calm, quiet and positive approach from the First Aider will invariably draw the same reaction from the casualty.

Don't lie to the victim. Play down the negative elements and play up the positives. Direct the victim. Ask about the incident. What? When? Where?. Why? Who? and How?

After getting as much information as possible change the subject, but occasionally repeat questions such as, where are you from and where are you going? These may help to determine if the casualty is responding or if they are becoming confused.

Most First Aiders and rescuers perform very well at incidents, even when they are confronted by unpleasantness and distasteful scenes. When the Police and/or MRT arrive hand the casualty over to the rescue services, then break the link with the casualty formally. Don't just let the rescue services barge you out of the way. Equally don't be obstructive. Tell them everything you know then step back and let them get on with it.

6.1.17. Dealing With Death

As First Aiders we are not in a position to decide if a casualty has died during treatment. It is imperative that you continue treatment to the best of your ability until advised otherwise by the rescue services, preferably a doctor.

If you have found an obviously dead casualty, do all the checks above and confirm that they are not in deep hypothermia. Cover the body and don't let bystanders interfere. Look after yourself by making notes about what you have found and what you have done. If there is no one else around mark the area and go for help. You are a key witness.

Apart from your checks and possibly ABC, do not move the body. You will probably be feeling quite low so share your feelings with someone. Guard your notes and when the mountain rescue team arrive tell them you have some notes. They will direct you to the police control point where you will be asked to give a statement and hand over your notes. These will be important for the inquest. If you have taken photos of the scene as evidence then hand the film over to the Police too.

Hand the body over to the rescue team honourably and with dignity. Tell them what you found and what you have done, then let the rescue services get on with their job. Incidents are very stressful, so once you have done this stand back and take stock.

After all incidents, no matter what the outcome, it will help you enormously to talk through the experience. Whatever you do don't bottle it all up. Delayed shock may hit you several hours after the event. It is normal to feel upset. Whatever the situation was during the incident your emotions should be of satisfaction that you did a good job.

Finally, there is a small risk that you could pick up infection from the casualty. If you are worried have a chat with the medical staff on the ground and then arrange to see your own GP. You should seek advice if there has been blood to blood contact.

6.1.18. First Aid Training

First aid courses run, or approved by St John Ambulance Association, The British Red Cross and St Andrew's Ambulance Association are recommended.

Alternatively, first aid at work courses governed by The Health and Safety (First Aid) Regulations 1981, are excellent but geared up for the work place rather than the outdoors. If you are a keen mountaineer consider attending one of the following;

- Basic First Aid In Mountaineering.
- Rescue and Emergency Care, run by various centres or the British Association Of Ski Patrollers (BASP).

6.1.19. Duty Of Care

A civil action for negligence (Cattley v St, John Ambulance Brigade 1988) against one of St, John Ambulance Brigade's First Aiders failed. The judge ruled that the individual had acted entirely in accordance with properly accepted First Aid practice (Mod. Law Rev 1990 53).

Legally, properly accepted first aid practice is that which is approved by the Voluntary Aid Societies for publication in their First Aid Manual, and which is used for training the First Aider.

6.1.20. First Aid Kits

First aid kit check lists are at Appendix E

6.2. Cold And Heat Injuries

6.2.0. Introduction

Cold and heat injuries are all preventable. Many have their origin in poor preparation, training and equipment. Unfortunately, many experienced and well equipped parties succumb to these injuries because they fail to recognise or acknowledge the conditions which lead to them, or worse, they have the equipment in their rucksacks but fail to use it.

6.2.1. Hypothermia

A person may be described as hypothermic when their core temperature drops from its constant of 37°C to below 35°C.

Body core temperature is constant at 37°C.
Hands, feet and skin temperature are constant at about 33-35°C.

When body core drops to;

- **36°C** shivering may begin.
- **35°C** there is numbness in hands, shivering mild to severe.
- **34°C** shivering is intense. Movement is slow and difficult. There is mild confusion and stumbling.
- **32°C** shivering becomes violent, speech is difficult. The casualty becomes sluggish, stumbles frequently and may show signs of depression.
- **30°C** shivering may stop. Exposed skin may be blue and puffed up. The casualty is unable to walk, they are confused, irrational and incoherent.
- **Below 30°C** muscles are severely rigid. The casualty may be semi-conscious, both pulse and breathing are slow. The casualty's pupils can still dilate.
- **Below 28°C** the casualty becomes unconscious, pulse and breathing become erratic and may be difficult to detect. Death may follow.

6.2.2. Contributory Factors

- Cold
- Wet
- Wind chill
- Exhaustion (tired and hungry)
- Low morale
- Effects of drugs
- Injury
- Over estimation of group ability
- Poor planning

6.2.3. Preventing Hypothermia

- Using proper clothing and equipment.
- Carrying and eating enough food and drink.
- Carrying and using emergency equipment.
- Ability and fitness.
- Awareness of prevailing conditions.

6.2.4. Signs & Symptoms Of Hypothermia

The initial stage of hypothermia is exposure. The casualty may notice;

- Sensation of cold, shivering and discomfort.
- Cramp in legs, pins and needles in hands.

If not treated exposure develops into hypothermia

- Unexpected or unreasonable behaviour.
- Complains of cold and tiredness.
- Physical and mental lethargy.
- Slurring of speech.
- Violent physical or verbal outbursts.
- Lacks muscular coordination.
- Moves erratically and may stumble frequently.
- Blurred vision.
- Uncontrollable and frequently violent shivering bouts.
- Loss of consciousness/coma/death.

6.2.5. Treating Hypothermia

Exposure. Seek shelter, lighten the load and rest. A hot drink and a chocolate bar (or similar) will invariably cheer the casualty. Give the casualty an extra layer of warm clothes and when they are feeling better walk them off the mountain to safety. If they are unable or unwilling to walk then treat them as for hypothermia.

Hypothermia. Stop, seek or build a shelter. Prevent further heat loss by insulating the ground. Add extra warm layers, do not remove wet clothing as this often makes the casualty worse. Then put the casualty in a sleeping bag inside a bivi bag, survival bag or group shelter.

Give warm (not hot) drinks and some sugary food.

Calm and reassure the casualty. Put a fit person in with the casualty. Monitor continuously (Observation Chart). Send for assistance as soon as possible. Hypothermia is very serious.

The pulse and breathing may be very difficult to detect. Do not forget the rest of the group. They will start deteriorating too. Keep them busy and their morale up.

> **Look after yourself . Don't become a casualty.**

The Dilemma. Having to choose between two equally hazardous alternatives, do we attempt to evacuate or do we stop and treat the condition and spend the night out?

Hypothermia casualties must be treated with great care because the slightest jolt could trigger heart defibrillation and cardiac arrest.

6.2.6. Frostbite.

The freezing or partial freezing of parts of the body, usually the extremities (face, hands and feet). It is either;

SUPERFICIAL. Dead white areas appear, no blisters.
DEEP. Blistering, the tissue under the blister dies and is lost.

Causes. Combinations of cold, windchill, moisture and restricted circulation.

Symptoms. Feeling of cold and pain, white waxy patches on the skin, insensitive skin, skin may stiffen or harden. The onset of frostbite can be reversed. Insensitive skin may indicate deep frostbite.

Because frost bitten extremities are frozen the casualty will be able to walk to medical aid. Once the injury thaws the casualty will be in severe pain and will be unable to walk.

Prevention.
- Knowledge of the contributory factors and recognition.
- Dress for the weather conditions and carry spare clothing.
- Avoid sweating, and put on extra clothing when you stop.
- Continuously check the hands, feet, toes and face for signs and symptoms.
- Seek shelter before the onset of exhaustion.
- Eat well and take plenty of liquid.
- Observe the rules for entering snow shelters and tents.
- Keep your feet clean and dry.(carry spare socks and gloves).
- Keep an eye on the others in the group.

Treatment.
- Seek shelter.
- Carefully dry the affected part. Do not rub.
- Face. Place a warm hand, mitten or other protection on the affected part.
- Hands. Place under armpits inside clothes or in the crutch.
- Feet. Remove boots and put on dry socks. Place the affected part somewhere warm (companion's arm pit or crotch).
- Elevate the affected part to alleviate swelling.
- Take warm food and drink.
- In all cases continue to warm the affected part until normal colour and sensitivity returns.
- Injuries which do not respond to treatment are very serious and evacuation must be made.

Do not rub the affected part, pick or burst blisters, use ointments, apply direct heat (stoves or hot water) and do not give alcohol or cigarettes. During recovery the casualty will experience severe pain.

6.2.7. Trench Foot

Trench foot occurs when the feet or hands are exposed to damp and near freezing conditions for prolonged periods.

Symptoms. The skin on the affected part will be waxy and white, swollen and painful. There may be numbness and tingling.

Treatment and prevention as for frostbite. Use foot powder and dry socks.

6.2.8. Snow Blindness

Occurs when the eyes are exposed to ultra violet (UV) light.

Symptoms. May appear several hours after exposure.
- Eye irritation and dry feeling as though they were full of grit. Severity depends on length of exposure.
- Swelling of the eyelids and excessive watering.
- Blindness for several hours or even days in very serious cases.
- Severe headaches, nausea and sunburn.

Prevention. Wear snow goggles even when overcast. Goggles must be correctly fitted and prevent light entering from the sides, above and below. If snow goggles are not available improvise by cutting slits in a piece of card or other suitable material. Eyes must be protected at all costs.

Treatment. Seek shelter. The casualty should be kept in the best shade available. Cool eyes with water or a cold compress. Do not allow the casualty to rub the eyes. If the eyes become infected or recovery is slow seek medical assistance.

6.2.9. Heat Injuries - Factors & Prevention

Heat injuries occur when the air temperature is the same as the body temperature, the body can no longer radiate heat away. As sweat evaporates it cools the skin down but when the air is very humid evaporation cannot take place and the body begins to overheat. Working in these conditions causes rapid over heating as the muscles continue to produce heat leading to varying levels of heat injury.

Factors leading to heat injuries are;
- High air temperature and humidity.
- Prolonged or heavy physical activity.
- Dehydration caused by failure to take sufficient water in.
- Excess alcohol or hangover.
- Affects of other drugs or illness.

Prevention of heat injuries;
- Frequent planned water stops.
- Regulate physical activity to cooler parts of day.
- Acclimatisation by increasing workload daily.
- Dehydration causes yellow to deep orange urine. The darker the colour the greater the level of dehydration.
- A good indicator of when the casualty is fit to move again is when their urine returns to its normal clear or pale yellow.
- Taking salt tablets is not recommended.

6.2.10. Fainting & Cramps

These are warning signs of the onset of more serious heat injuries.

Fainting. The casualty faints and recovers within seconds. Rest and give plenty of liquids. Modify activity and seek shade.

Cramps. The muscle contracts and is very painful and cannot be straightened. Rest, massage and stretch the affected limb. Give plenty of water, use commercially available electrolytes if available.

6.2.11. Heat Exhaustion

This is now beginning to get serious. The body cannot dissipate heat fast enough. The casualty may not notice the onset of the condition. Awareness of the conditions which lead to heat injuries is vital.

Signs
- Pale clammy skin
- Sweating (may be profuse)
- Rapidly weakening pulse and breathing

Symptoms
- Loss of appetite
- Thirst

- Nausea
- Headache and dizziness
- Weakness and tiredness

Treatment
- Lie the casualty in a cool shaded place.
- Give plenty of water, use commercially available electrolytes if available.
- Rest until signs and symptoms have completely cleared.

6.2.12. Heat Stroke

Heat stroke is life threatening and must be treated with the greatest of urgency. The body temperature is 41°C or greater.

Signs
- There is a full bounding pulse
- The casualty has hot, dry and very red skin
- The casualty may experience a rapidly deteriorating pulse rate and breathing
- Unconsciousness may follow rapidly

Symptoms
- Weakness and confussion
- Irritable and restless
- Dizziness and headache

Treatment
- Body temperature must be reduced rapidly.
- Place casualty in a cool shaded place and remove clothing.
- Raise feet.
- Spray with cool water or use wet towels especially to the head, neck, armpits and groin.
- Vigorous fanning will help.
- If the casualty is conscious give sips of water.
- Arrange to evacuate to hospital with great urgency.
- Continue to cool the casualty until arrival at hospital, monitor their responses continuously and give this information to the medical staff.

6.2.13. Burns

The seriousness of a burn depends on how deep it penetrates the skin and on the area of the body it covers.

First Degree Burns. Sun burn or flash burns. Causes reddening of skin and may be sensitive or painful and may begin to peel later. Recovery is always complete.

Second Degree Burns. Such as a scold, is a deeper and more extensive burn. Liquid filled blisters develop very quickly and are very painful. Clothing may be charred and stuck to the burn site. Secondary infection may develop quickly if untreated.

Third Degree Burns. Electric shock burns or contact with a very hot object. The skin is completely burned and there is a hole. The skin surrounding the site may be white, black or brown. The casualty feels no pain as all the blood vessels and nerves are destroyed. First and second degree burns may surround the site. The burn site is sterile but may become infected quickly. There is a large and rapid loss of fluid which may include blood.

6.2.14. Treating Burns

For all burns;
- Remove the source of heat.
- If the casualty is on fire lay them down and roll them in anything to douse the flames.
- Cool the affected part for 20-30 minutes by submerging in cold water. Alternatively, hold the affected part under running water.
- Do not attempt to remove clothing charred to the burn site.
- Cover with a dry, non adhesive, non absorbant dressing.
- Cover with a plastic sheet or place inside a polythene bag.
- Elevate the affected limb if possible. (May be difficult).
- Treat for shock.
- It is beneficial to give warm sweet drinks.
- Do not apply any form of cream.
- Do not burst blisters or interfere with the burn site.
- Depending on the extent of the injury - evacuate to hospital (see 6.2.15 below).

- Any serious first and all second degree burns covering more than 1% of the body (size of the palm of your hand) must be seen by a doctor.
- All third degree burns must be treated in a hospital.
- Second degree burns greater than 9% will be followed by the rapid onset of shock.
- Evacuation must be done smoothly and moderately rapidly.

The Rule of 9's - For the purpose of assessing the extent of a burn each part of the body can be described thus,

Head & neck 9%

Chest 9%

Back 9%

Right arm 9%

Left arm 9%

Abdomen 9%

Lower back and buttocks 9%

Right leg

Left leg

Front 9% back 9%

Front 9% back 9%

1%

7. Access

7.0. Introduction

Access and conservation are a concern for us all. We must do all in our power to guard our rights and look after those regions which give us all so much pleasure. The codes of practice have been developed with the help of all who live and work there and all who visit. They are offered in a spirit of cooperation and to serve as a source of advice.

7.1. Rights Of Way - The Law

Rights of way are;

- **Public Footpaths.** Accessible on foot only.
- **Bridleways.** Accessible by foot, horseback, and pedal cycle. Cyclists must give way to horses and pedestrians. Vehicles, including horse drawn carriages are not permitted.
- **Byways**. All traffic may use these, many are roads used as public paths (RUPP). All have notices at access points stating that they are byways. Some may have local restrictions.

On the right of way you can take;
- A pram, push chair or wheel chair.
- A dog on a lead and under control.
- A short diversion around obstructions.

The existence of a public right of way is recorded on the definitive map held and maintained by the local highways authority. Rights of way shown on OS maps are based on these definitive maps.

Obstructions, dangerous animals, harassment and misleading signs on public rights of way are illegal. Landowners and farmers must not disturb or obstruct rights of way along the edge of fields. If the right of way crosses a large field the line must be made apparent.

It is inevitable that some rights of way will be disturbed but they must be restored within a reasonable time, normally within 24 hours, or up to 14 days if this is the first time the ground is being ploughed. The surface must be made good so that walkers and horse riders are not inconvenienced.

The land owner can require you to leave land to which you have no right of access. The only exception is when you are making a detour around an illegal obstruction.

"Trespassers will be prosecuted" is a misleading sign. But the land owner can sue you if you knowingly enter private property without good cause.

It is normally in the landowners interest to restore rights of way because local authorities normally restore them to considerably larger than the legal minimum.

If you encounter a problem on a right of way inform your local authority footpaths officer as soon as possible. Please give;

- The date of the problem
- A 6 figure grid reference or a marked map if possible
- Details of the problem

7.2. The Country Code

The Country Code is a practical guide with the interests of all users and local inhabitants in mind. Conservation and access form an integral part of the code.

- Respect the countryside, all its users and its inhabitants.
- Take care on country roads and other rights of way.
- Use gates and stiles to cross walls, hedges and fences.
- Close gates after use.
- Keep to public rights of way across farmland and do not tamper with farm machinery, buildings, animals or crops.
- Keep animals (dogs and horses) under control.
- Protect wildlife, plants and trees.
- Safeguard water supplies.
- Take your litter home with you.
- Guard against risk of fire.
- Avoid unnecessary noise.

7.3. The Mountain Code

In addition to the country code the Mountain Code offers specific advice to all users of the mountainous regions of the UK. The spirit and principles of the code are equally applicable anywhere in the world.

- Have the correct clothing and equipment, keep it serviceable and know how to use it.
- Carry a first aid kit and know how to use it.
- Know what rescue facilities exist in the area you are visiting.
- Be proficient at navigation and ensure you are fit enough for the task at hand. Trust your compass.
- Travelling alone is inadvisable for the inexperienced.
- Leave details of your intentions and route with a responsible person and report back when you have returned.
- If you are not using official campsites seek permission from the land owner and avoid open fires.
- Do not pollute fresh water.
- Avoid game shooting parties.
- Lead only climbs and walks which you are competent to.
- Do not throw stones. If you dislodge stones onto people below warn them by shouting "Below".
- Have the latest local forecast.
- Do not hesitate to turn back if conditions deteriorate.
- If there is snow and ice around, understand the local conditions. Only go out when you have the essential winter skills and equipment.

7.4. Useful Addresses

The British Mountaineering Council (BMC). 177-179 Burton Road, West Didsbury, Manchester, M20 2BB. 0161 445 4747. Email: office@thebmc.co.uk

Mountaineering Council of Scotland. The Old Granery. West Mill Street. Perth PH1 5QP 01738 638227

Mountaineering Council of Ireland. House of Sport, Longmile Road, Dublin 12. 003531 509845

United Kingdom Mountain Training Board (UKMTB).
Siabod Cottage. Capel Curig. Gwynedd. LL24 0ET. 01690 720314

The Mountain Leader Training Board (MLTB)
177-179 Burton Road. Manchester. M20 2BB. 0161 445 4747.
Email info@mltb.org Website: www.mltb.org

The Scottish Mountain Leader Training Board (SMLTB).
Glenmore. Aviemore, Inverness-shire. PH22 1QU. 01479 861248

The Welsh Mountain Leader Training Board (WMLTB)
Plas Menai. Llanfairisgaer. Carnarfon. Gwynedd. LL55 1UE
01248 670964

Northern Ireland Mountain Leader Training Board (NIMLTB). Sports Council For Northern Ireland, House of Sport, Upper Malone Road, Belfast. 01232 381222

Ramblers Association. Camelford House, 87-89 Albert Embankment. London SE1 7TW. 0207 359 8500

Ramblers Association (Scotland) Crusader House, Haig Business Park, Markinch, Fife, KYY 6AQ. 01592 611177

The National Trust. PO Box 39, Bromley, Kent. BR1 3XL. 0181 464 1111

The National Trust For Scotland. 5 Charlotte Square, Edinburgh. EH2 4DU. 0131 226 5922

John Muir Trust. 41 Commercial Street, Leith. Edinburgh. EH6 7JD. 0131 554 9101

The Royal Meteorological Society. 104 Oxford Road, Reading. RG1 7LJ (For A4 pads of Met maps)

7.5. References & Further Reading

Barton & Wright (2000) **A Chance In A Million** 2nd Ed Scottish Mountaineering Club.

Bollen S (1989) **First Aid On Mountains** BMC.

Cliffe P (1991) **Mountain Navigation** 4th Ed Cordee

Cliffe P (1988) **Alpinism** –An Introduction To Safe alpine Mountaineering

Deegan P (2002) **The Mountain Travellers Handbook** The BMC

First Aid Manual 7th Edition (1997) Dorling Kindersley

Fyffe & Peters (1997) **The Handbook Of Climbing** Pelham Books.

Graydon D (1997) **Mountaineering - Freedom Of The Hills** The Mountaineers Books

Jones I.W. Dr (1994). **First Aid In Mountaineering** 3rd Ed St, John Ambulance Brigade In Wales.

Tippett J (2001) **Navigation For Walkers** Cordee

Langmuir E (1995) **Mountaincraft & Leadership** 3rd Ed MLTB & Scottish Sports Council.

Lentz et al (1996) **Mountaineering First Aid** 4th Ed. The Mountaineers Books.

Letham L (2001) **GPS Made Easy** Using Global Positioning Systems In the Outdoors 3rd Ed Rocky Mountain Books

Luebben C (1995) **Knots For Climbers** Chockstone Press

MacNae A, Last A and Newton A (2000) **Safety on Mountains** BMC

McClung & Schaerer (1993) **The Avalanche Handbook** The Mountaineers Books.

Meyer K (1994) **How To Shit In The Woods** 2nd Ed Ten Speed Press (USA).

MLTB (Summer) (1993) **Guidance Notes For Candidates, Trainers and Assessors**.

Mountain & Cave Rescue Handbook (1994) The Mountain Rescue Committee.

Moran M (1998) **Scotlands Winter Mountains** David & Charles.

Thomas M (1995) **Weather For Hillwalkers and Climbers** Allan Sutton Publishing Ltd.

Wilkerson (1986) **Hypothermia, Frostbite and Other Cold Injuries** The Mountaineers Books.

These and many other good books on outdoor activities can be found in the Cordee stocklist available free from;

Cordee. 3a De Montfort Street, Leicester, LE1 7HD.
email: sales@cordee.co.uk
web: www.cordee.co.uk

Appendices

These appendices are intended for your personal use. Feel free to copy them and waterproof them as required. The intention is for you to adapt the information to suit your own needs.

These are for your own use only, please respect this request.

Appendix A. Accident Report Form

Todays Date: | **Time**

Grid reference

Location. Give the messengers a map which you have personally marked. Give a description of the ground. Use a sketch map. Include prominent features and location of casualty.

Describe The Incident. Include where you were going and where you have just come from. What you were doing and what happened. If the casualty is not from your group describe the circumstances in which you found them.

Injured Person(s) Male or Female?

Name	Age

General Condition. Good/Fair/Serious. **Unconscious** Yes/No If yes for how long. (Use the observation charts)

Nature Of Injuries. Give a description of each injury, i.e. where it is, what is it and what have you done about it.

On The Scene Plan. List all the members of your party remaining with the casualty. Have they got enough gear and are they okay to bivi out over night. **OR** if you have decided to attempt to evacuate the casualty say how you are doing it and where you are aiming for.

Party Leader

Names of all the messengers

Casualty Name   Date

Time Observation Started   Record every 10 Mins

	Time	0	1 0	2 0	3 0	4 0	5 0	6 0	7 0	8 0	9 0
Eyes	Open Spontaneously										
	Open to Speech										
	Open to painful stimulus										
	No Response										
Movement	Obeys Commands										
	Responds to Pain										
	No Response										
Speech	Normal										
	Confused										
	Inappropriate Words										
	Incomprehensible										
	No Response										
Pulse	111-120+										
	101-110										
	91-100										
	81-90										
	71-80										
	61-70										
	51-60										
Breathing	41-50+										
	31-40										
	21-30										
	11-20										
	1-10										

In the relevant box in each category enter;

- **Eyes, Movement & Speech.** Tick in relevant box
- **Pulse**. **W** Weak, **S** Strong, **R** Regular, **I** Irregular, **B** Bounding
- **Breathing**. **Q** - Quiet, **N** - Noisy, **E** - Easy, **D** - Difficult

This chart plus the notes below form an invaluable record for the medical services. They should go to hospital with the casualty. (Use a separate chart for each casualty.)

Observation Chart Notes

Casualty Name

1. A Brief description of accident or illness.
2. A brief description of the injuries.
3. Time and description of any treatment given.
4. Note how long the casualty was unconscious for.
5. Time that their condition changed.
6. Duration of any fits.

Appendix C Personal Timing & Pacing Tables

Timings
Minutes : Seconds

Distance walked (Meters) Surface	50	100	150	500	1000
Hard level surface					
Variable, undulating					
Firm Snow					
Deep snow, steep slope					

Pacing (Your own double paces)

One complete pace is counted each time the left foot strikes the ground. (Right if you prefer.)

Distance (Meters) Surface	50	100	150	500	1000
Hard level surface					
Variable, undulating					
Firm Snow					
Deep snow, steep slope					

Accurately measure 100m on a flat firm surface. First time yourself over the 100m then count how many paces you took. Fill in the relevent boxes. Repeat this exercise for 50m and 150m. From these results calculate the 500m and 1000m distances.

If you are feeling energetic you can repeat the exercise on the different types of terrain.

Appendix D1. Leader's Equipment List

W Winter. S Summer opt Optional	Low Camp	High Camp	Low Walk	High Walk
Length of 9mm Rope				
Group 1st Aid Kit				
Extra Emergency Rations				
Extra Fleece				
Group Shelter (GESU)				
Red Smoke				
Flares				

Appendix D2. Summer Equipment List

	Low Camp	High Camp	Low Walk	High Walk
RuckSack & Liner				
Map & Compass				
Whistle				
Watch				
Note Book & Pencil				
Pocket Knife				
Torch + Spare Batteries				
First Aid Kit Personal				
Waterproof Jacket				
Waterproof Trousers				
Survival Bag				
Boots				
Socks				
Trousers				
Shirt or similar				
Fleece or Sweater				
Emergency Rations.				
Day Rations				
............Days Rations				
Hat & Gloves				
Sleeping Bag & Liner				
Sleeping Mat				
Stove + Fuel				
KFS and Mug				
Plate or Bowl				

Cooking Pots				
Method of Ignition				
Tent				
Camera				
Small Radio				
Binoculars				
Scourer & Cloth				
Detergent				
Toilet Requisites				
Sun Glasses				

Appendix D3. Winter Equipment

Equipment	Low Camp	High Camp	Low walk	High Walk
Thermals				
Neck Warmer				
Gaiters				
Overmitts				
Balaclava				
Extra Fleece				
Ice Axe				
Crampons				
Snow Goggles				
Snow Shovel				
Sleeping Bag				

Appendix E. First Aid Kit List

Personal First Aid Kit. Each Individual should have one of these. Normally best kept in a waterproof container on the individual or in the top pocket of their rucksack.

Aspirin or paracetamol (own use)   Personal medication
1 crepe bandage 10cm x 4.5m   Assorted plasters
1 Melolin dressing 10x10cm 1   Triangular bandage
2 Melolin dressings 5x5cm   4 small safety pins
1 compressed dressing

Additional items stowed outside the first aid kit.

Lip salve   Insect repellent
Sun cream   After sun cream

Group First Aid Kit (Carried by leader or other trained First Aider). Leaders and other First Aiders in the group are not to carry anything which they have not been trained to use. Only medical professionals are licensed to administer drugs. There should be no drugs in this kit nor should you offer anyone drugs from your own first aid kit.

Light weight container (Strong and waterproof)
Plastic bag(s) for medical waste   A pair of strong scissors
Small pack of surgical gloves   Surgical antiseptic wipes
Airway (Size 3 for general use)   A small torch
2 crepe bandages 10cm x 4.5m   1 scalpel blade
2 compressed Dressings   2 triangular bandages
2 Melolin dressings 10x10cm   1 roll zinc oxide plaster
4 Melolin dressings 5x5cm   Forceps (Sharp ended)
Safety pins (Assorted Sizes)   Roll non stick dressing
1 pack butterfly sutures or steristrips

As a general rule use the casualty's first aid kit before your own or the group kit.

Most of this equipment may be bought in any High Street chemists.

Appendix F. Contact Card

> Complete this card and leave it with a reliable contact.
> Use the back of this card for additional notes if required

1. Todays date
2. Time due back
3. Card left at/with

4. Names of people in group   Level of experience

a.

b.

c.

d.

e.

f.

5. We have todays weather forecast   Yes/No

6. Outline of days route

Starting at
via
via
via
via
via
via
via
via
Finishing at

7. Equipment In The Group

Map	Compass	Whistle	Torch
Bivibags	Waterproofs	Warm Gear	Flask
Extra Food	Hat And Gloves	First Aid Kit	Rope
Ice Axe	Crampons	Sleeping Bag	

Appendix G. Notes On Party Leadership

Leadership is essentially a lonely but selfless activity which requires strength of character, personality and humility. A leaders concern is for the group first and foremost. The quality of their experience depends on the quality of your accumulated experience, knowledge and leadership style.

A Leaders 3 primary tasks are;
- Complete responsibility for everyone in your group
- Achieving a balance between
  - Real or imagined danger   potentially exciting
  - Total safety   potentially boring
- Continuously weigh up risk factors, consider likely consequences of actions and alternative s options .

But leadership is far more complex than this. You also need to;
- Manage the whole day including
  - Planning and preparation prior to the trip
  - Running the activity
  - Ensuring that everyone has had a good day and that they want to come back again
- See things from the parties point of view
- Give direction and purpose
- Continuously encourage and inspire the group
- Communicate with everyone in the group by;
  - Passing on mountain skills
  - Discussing the physical mountain environment
  - Look at flora and fauna
  - Discuss the human aspect of the mountains
  - Spend 50% of your time listening to what your group have to say.

These are just a few questions which you may like to ask yourself continuously;
- Why do I want to be a leader?
- What am I getting out of the experience?
- Is the trip within my own level of competence?

Planning and Preparation
- Who am I planning this venture for?
- Did I use PPPPPPP and KISS?
- How fit is each individual?
- Am I being too ambitious for the group?
- Will the venture be demanding enough?
- Is there a balance?
- Am I aware of all the factors that may cause a problem during the venture and what strategies do I have to cope with them?

Briefing The Group
- Does everyone know what the aim of the venture is?
- Is everyone adequately equipped?
- Has everyone got enough food and drink?
- Do the group know what to do if I become injured?

My Skills During The Venture
- Shall I lead from the front, middle or back, can I use all these strategies?
- Can I communicate with everyone in my group?
- Am I enthusiastic and encouraging everyone equally?
- Am I continuously observing the group and their reactions to the experience including the weather and the knowledge which they are acquiring?

How Do I deal With The Group During The Venture?
- Am I being flexible or too rigid?
- Am I aware of all the characters in the group?
  - Are any of them likely to be a problem?
  - If so, when and where can I avoid it?
  - Who are the boisterous ones and how do I manage them?
- Is everyone aware of what is going on;
  - Where we are?
  - Where we are going?
  - What our intentions are?
- Is there anything which I must avoid doing or saying?

A successful day out should encourage all who attended to come back for more.